BEYOND SPIRITUAL BIGOTRY

· AN EX-FUNDAMENTALIST RE-EXAMINES HIS FAITH ·

RANDY LANDIS

Outskirts Press, Inc.
Denver, Colorado

Outskirts Press, Inc.
http://www.outskirtspress.com

ISBN: 978-1-4327-2216-6

Outskirts Press and the "OP" logo are trademarks belonging to Outskirts Press, Inc.

PRINTED IN THE UNITED STATES OF AMERICA

CONTENTS

BEFORE GOING BEYOND
A BRIEF INTRODUCTION

The nightmarish excesses of the George W. Bush era have been (and will be) better documented by those more familiar with them than I. The specific purpose of this book is to focus on the underpinnings of one group of people who helped make this nightmare possible and who, for the most part, supported Bush to the bitter end. I refer to fundamentalist Christians. I was once one of them.

This writing is not a laboriously footnoted academic exercise stating why literal Christianity is objectively false. It is, rather, a series of messages (sermons, if you will) organized in a way to present the information contained in them as clearly as possible. I share two simple concepts with very low standards of proof- the first being that all illustrations of God and all forms of spirituality deserve equal respect. The second is that political and religious dogma which threatens our planet must be critically examined. If the theme of this book could be summed up in one sentence, it would be this: people do not fly planes into buildings because they worship the wrong God, they fly planes into buildings because they have convinced themselves that others worship the wrong God.

I would like to thank the following friends and associates who encouraged, supported and/or debated me as I prepared the chapters which follow. A few even attended church with me as I worked on chapter seven. They are: John Skalman, Darcy Chambers, Dave Ward, Jorge Barrera, Sara Kasteleyn, Soren Blanc, Jim Gallas, Phil

Harris, John Landis, Leslie Smith, Tony Deutsch, Curtis Quay and Kevin Mahoney.

Randy Landis

March 2009

CHAPTER 1
CHANGING THE PAST

Beyond False History

Over the course of nearly 2000 years the label "Christian" has meant many different things. When asked if I would like to become one in the summer of 1995, it conjured a very different image than the same word creates in my mind today. It was then that I decided to make what was called a decision for Christ. The net effect of that decision was three years of indoctrination in what I now call "the Overstory."

By the end of the summer of 1995 I thought I was among a caring group of people who were leading me from uncertainty toward something they called salvation. A clear perspective on human history and humanity's future was promised through the study of Bible stories and prophecy. Three years later, I saw that the "personal relationship with Jesus Christ" I was promised had amounted to a wholesale brainwashing. I have gradually come to see the tenets of my former faith for what they really are: a potent mixture of false history, contrived biography, book idolatry, ancient mythology, fear and right-wing propaganda. The mix is topped off with the Armageddon agenda which now threatens the very planet we all share.

If an individual's right to wave his fist ends at the face of another the same outlook should apply to the practice of his or her religion. For example, a group of sorcerers living in a certain neighborhood have the right to embrace their teachings and practices as their own private business. It becomes the neighborhood's business once they begin to foul the air with noxious brews or ritually sacrifice neighborhood pets. In any context, individual or group behavior which threatens or abuses others is wrong. Anything which increases the likelihood of nuclear war or reckless management of our planet's resources is not a simple matter of personal faith. Religious fundamentalism which dismisses or demonizes the spirituality of others, no matter the book or teacher from which it is derived, crosses an unacceptable line.

The promotion of a history-ending struggle which will supposedly bring Jesus down from the sky is a threat to everyone with any other outlook. Behavior which is motivated by the notion that the world is in its last fleeting moments discourages the sane management of the earth's finite and dwindling resources. Before we blindly stumble to the end of the world it would help to take a step back and look at how humanity got to where it is in the first place. Western religion is substantially, though certainly not exclusively, responsible for the plight of our planet. Since we are not being offered accurate history by the fundamentalist movement I took it upon myself to discover objective answers to the following questions:

1. Can the history of Christianity be fairly summarized?

2. Has Christianity had a positive influence on human affairs?

3. How do modern fundamentalists distort historical truth?

A FOUR PART SUMMARY OF CHRISTIAN HISTORY

Since we are still not too far past the year 2000, it is convenient to present a summary of Christian history in four 500-year segments. This coincidentally flows well with the major periods of Christian history.

1 CE to 500 CE: Christianity Decides What It Is

Jesus of Nazareth was executed by the Roman Empire as a political criminal sometime around 28 CE. A small group of his followers lead by Peter then circulated a story that he had risen from the dead. It is no longer possible to determine whether they meant to spread the idea that Jesus had risen physically or in a strictly spiritual sense. For the first 50 years or so after Jesus was crucified word-of-mouth storytelling sustained the notions of a small group of Jews and a small but growing number of Gentiles who awaited Jesus' return from heaven.

Saul of Tarsus, now known as the Apostle Paul, wrote a series of letters between the years of 50 and 64 CE which survive as New Testament scripture today. Ironically, he would never have intended to write anything for posterity. Paul, like Peter, expected Jesus' return in a very short time. His epistles were merely last minute advice to a scattered group of pen pals. When the four Bible gospels were written, between 75 and 120 CE, scores of similar writings were also being produced.

For a variety of reasons, Christianity had evolved from a Jewish cult into a separate Gentile religion by the start of the second century. There were several factors behind this, but three stand out. The first was Paul's influence on the Christian movement. A Jew who possessed Roman citizenship, Paul thought that Gentiles should be included in the Kingdom of God. Too Gentile in his outlook for Jews and too Jewish to find protection from the Roman government, Paul was executed by the empire in the year 65 CE.

A second major factor in the Christian transition away from Judaism was the Roman-Jewish War of 66-70 CE, which saw the destruction of Jerusalem and the end of a Jewish homeland until the year 1948. The Gospel of Mark, completed by 75 CE, labors to clear Rome from guilt in the killing of Jesus. Mark's desire to avoid further stirring up Rome's wrath was shared by the authors of the three later Bible gospel accounts. In fact, Luke was actually a Gentile himself, underscoring the non-Jewish influence on the development of early Christian lore.

Finally, the Gentile-friendly door Paul opened invited the addition of pagan mythology to the stories being circulated about Jesus of Nazareth. What began as just another Jewish messiah cult soon included Gentile-flavored tales of virgin birth and a resurrecting hero. Legitimate Jews naturally shunned such images.

As first and second generation hearsay about Jesus died with the earliest Christians, a word-of mouth storytelling tradition was replaced in the second century by increased reliance upon writings. Different groups used different books and the question of which writings were acceptable and which were not was never officially settled until 393 CE. This will be examined in greater detail in chapter four.

By the early 200s Christianity had begun the transition from a troublesome cult to a familiar presence in Roman culture. By the year 300, those Christians promoting Jesus' resurrection as a literal, physical event had gained the upper hand in the new religion. Legitimate rival groups like the Gnostics, who saw the resurrection as a spiritual phenomenon, were labeled heretics.

As the Roman empire declined, the fanaticism associated with Christianity became attractive to a political leadership wanting to motivate its citizenry. The Emperor Constantine was especially impressed with the Christians, and in 313 he outlawed all persecution against them. Constantine's preference for the religion became obvious when Christian bishops were granted equal status to Roman Senators in the year 324, and his desire for uniform Christianity led to the Council of Nicea in 325. The Council officially spelled out the Trinity concept of God after a good deal of political maneuvering. The Nicene Creed stated that God the Father and Jesus the Son were "made of the same stuff" and added the phrase "we believe in the Holy Spirit."

The influence of the Church expanded during the final decades of the Roman Empire. In 380 the Emperor Flavius made Christianity the official state religion and by 435 so-called heretics were regularly executed. When the Western Roman Empire fell in 476, it's only surviving institution was the Catholic Church. It then took control, and Western civilization fell into a hellish decline which would last for centuries.

500 to 1000 CE: The Dark Ages

Not long after the Church stepped in to fill the void left by the fall of Imperial Rome progress in education, architecture, commerce, science and culture collapsed entirely. By the mid-500s education was available only to the priesthood. History was re-written by the Church and blind faith in its doctrines was enforced with a heavy hand. The cultures of pre-Christian Greece and Rome were degraded as "paganism." Roman aqueducts and irrigation systems vanished or fell into disrepair while the economy of Western Europe collapsed because the lending of money for interest was not allowed.

During the Dark Ages the Church became a highly profitable enterprise and the best place for ambitious men to pursue a career. Because of power and greed, crime and murder became a way of life in the church. The papacy was a coveted prize which changed hands frequently. Twelve Popes actually came to power during one twelve-year period between the years of 891 and 903.

Church authorities spent the Dark Ages jockeying for political and economic power. Alliances with political states were common, and bishops often held church and secular offices at the same time in the small post-Roman states. While this went on, the lives of common people were characterized by grim subsistence and blind faith in religious doctrine. The fear and ignorance created by Christianity itself were very effective promoters of the faith of the day.

1000 to 1500 CE: The Middle Ages

By the year 1000, European population growth was creating commerce in cities and towns. As this commerce expanded, information was passed more rapidly than during previous times. Regular

[5]

contact with Greek and Arab traders expanded the knowledge of people in Western Europe to the point that the Church began to feel threatened.

Church leaders decided to change the people's focus from secular knowledge to the fear of a religious enemy. In 1095 Pope Urban II called upon the knights of Europe to unite and march to Jerusalem to protect the holy land from Islamic threat. The response was the torture, decapitation and burning to death of Jews and Muslims. This was the start of 200 years of Holy Crusades. In 1204 Constantinople, the center of the Eastern Orthodox Church, was also pillaged and burned by agents of the Pope over differences in the observance of Easter.

A new program of spiritual terrorism began in 1231 when Pope Gregory IX started the Inquisition. Its purpose was to punish anyone criticizing the doctrines and practices of the Catholic Church. By 1245 the Pope officially excused all violence necessary to "enforce the faith." As many Inquisitors grew wealthy, the compassionate Catholic Franciscan Order of Friars complained to Rome. In response, Pope Martin V ordered the leveling of their village in 1315 where a number of Franciscan friars were executed for refusing to abandon their vow of poverty.

As terrible as the Inquisition was for enlightened Christians, it was far worse for European Jews. In 1391 the Archdeacon of Seville declared a holy war against them. Within a few decades the majority of Spanish Jews had been executed, deported or had forcibly converted to Christianity. Spanish Muslims faced the same treatment with similar results. Because it proved such an effective tool, the Inquisition enjoyed long-lasting popularity with Church leaders and was not abolished until 1834.

After denying the existence of witches for centuries, the Church reversed itself in 1320. Pope John XII announced a program to combat sorcery at that time, and those accused of offenses ranging from having sex with demons to flying through the air at night were arrested. In 1488 Pope Innocent VIII issued a call to the nations of Europe to rescue the Church from those practicing the arts of Satan. As a result, thousands of people were tortured or executed.

As the Middle Ages drew to a close the Catholic Church, while somewhat distracted by the Inquisition and witch hunting, continued its traditional pursuit of wealth. The European discovery of the Americas presented a vast new supply of both riches to plunder and souls to save. Unexpectedly, the very pursuit of profit which had been a large part of Christianity since the fall of Rome was about to cause the Church some serious problems.

1500 CE to the Present: Christianity Again Decides What It Is

A German friar known as Martin Luther began the Protestant Reformation in 1517. Offended by Church profiteering, Luther taught that the word of the Bible was more trustworthy than the dictates of the Pope. Finding support mainly among Northern Europeans tired of paying taxes to Rome, Luther's Reformation took hold and found new leaders in the likes of Switzerland's John Calvin and England's King Henry VIII. While the new Protestant churches divided and subdivided with fresh faces and new ideas, friction between Catholics and Protestants threw Europe into endless conflict. A particularly long-lasting example of Christian-on-Christian violence was the Thirty Years War. It involved Sweden, the Netherlands, France, England, Demark, several German states and the Holy Roman Empire and dragged on from 1616 to 1648.

European struggles over religion, wealth and political power were exported to the New World. Catholic Spain scored big first, forcing Christianity upon the natives of the Americas as it plundered their silver and gold. Catholic France and Protestant England also moved in, and with some of the English colonists came the religious fanaticism still thriving in North America today. Probably the best known of the English oddball groups, the Puritans, settled in Massachusetts in the 1630s. When the United States established its independence from England in 1776 and later ratified its Constitution and Bill of Rights, great care was taken to limit the influence of the Puritans and other fanatic and intolerant Christian groups.

The splintering and re-splintering of various Protestant sects has been ongoing. With the Bible as the final word on all matters and no Catholic Church to provide oversight, any charismatic individual with a fresh spin on the scriptures can set out on his own. While notable non-Americans like England's John Wesley (whose Methodist movement separated from the Church of England in 1784) had an impact, by the dawn of the nineteenth century the United States had emerged as the clear world leader in radical Christian ideas and activity. It is a dubious distinction America has never relinquished. During the 1800s America gave birth to a wide array of new and offbeat Christian groups including the Church of Jesus Christ of Latter-day Saints (Mormons), Seventh-day Adventists, Christian Scientists and Jehovah's Witnesses.

The technical and scientific progress of the twentieth century provided a colorful backdrop for the ever-widening divide between religious fanaticism and empirical knowledge. The advent of motorized flight in 1903, the atomic bomb in 1945 and manned lunar exploration in 1969 hastened new ideas about matter, energy, time and space. Two World Wars and the Cold War which followed provided fertile ground for successive generations of end times speculators. Theologians partial to guesswork found eager readership for books providing specific predictions about Jesus' ever-imminent return.

As reasonable Christians began to realize that the Bible was neither a literal science text nor a consistently reliable source of history, America stayed true to its heritage of fringe Christian innovation. While the 1960s hippie youth movement fueled an openness about everything from spirituality to sexuality, by the end of the decade hippie Christianity had also come upon the scene. Blending an eccentric mix of Christian rock music, come-as-you-are fashion and Bible-pounding fundamentalism, the Jesus Freak phenomenon has experienced huge growth over the past 40 years.

Probably the most influential of the groups making up this new Christianity has been the "non-denominational" Calvary Chapel movement. Still-active Pastor Chuck Smith began the church in Costa Mesa, California in 1965. While total membership numbers are not available Calvary Chapel now includes over 600 churches worldwide, with at least 400 congregations in the United States. From 1995 to 1998 I was a member of one of these churches, Mission Valley Christian Fellowship of San Diego. During my time there I recall a young woman earnestly telling me "I used to be a Catholic, but now I am a Christian."

The Roman Catholic Church, which emerged from Christianity's first 500 years as Western Europe's only significant Christian body, remains it's largest single group worldwide. The past 500 years, however, have seen the emergence of a Christianity where an individual's decision to establish what is called a personal relationship with God has increasingly replaced the earlier tradition of strict adherence to the dictates of clergy. Ex-Catholics and former mainstream Protestants alike swell the ranks of the post-1960s Jesus Movement, a major component in present-day right wing politics. For those interested in further examining organized Christianity's 2000 years of abuses and excesses, I recommend Helen Ellerbe's book "The Dark Side of Christian History."

THE INFLUENCE OF CHRISTIANITY ON HUMAN AFFAIRS

No reasonably informed Christian of any denomination will deny the fact that evil people have sometimes led Christianity astray as Western history has unfolded. It is also impossible to deny that terrible events have sometimes occurred in Jesus' name over the course of the past two thousand years. Nevertheless, the modern Catholic apologist will promote the idea that the Church has policed itself and made necessary corrections as it went along. Protestants, by nature critical of the Catholic Church, will point to the sixteenth century Reformation as a starting point for the ongoing elimination of organized Christianity's shortcomings.

On the whole, the entire course of Christian history has been a pretty dismal affair. While certain individuals have undoubtedly used the teachings of Jesus as a pathway to enlightenment, Christian organizations generally have been anything but a positive force on humanity. I use an illustration called the 100 Mile Christian Walk to demonstrate this historical truth. Using each 20 years of the past 2000 as one mile, the following signposts mark the journey:

MILE 1: Jesus of Nazareth is executed by the Roman Empire (Circa 28 CE).

MILE 18: The writings which appear in the Bible are finally listed (367 CE).

MILE 19: Christianity becomes the official religion of the Roman Empire (380 CE).

MILE 24: The Western Roman Empire falls, Europe begins to slip into the Dark Ages (476 CE).

MILE 55: The Church begins the barbaric Crusades (1095 CE).

MILE 61: The shockingly violent Inquisition is initiated (1231 CE).

MILE 66: Church sanctioned witch hunting officially begins (1320 CE).

MILE 76: Anti-Semite Martin Luther begins the Protestant Reformation (1519 CE).

MILE 82: The marathon Catholic versus Protestant Thirty Years War finally ends (1648 CE).

MILE 85: Protestant Puritans execute 20 people for witchcraft in Massachusetts (1692 CE).

MILE 92: The Southern Baptist Convention forms to support slavery in the U.S. (1845 CE).

MILE 98: The modern Jesus Movement begins on the American West Coast (circa 1965 CE).

Modern fundamentalists are frequently heard calling for a return to traditional values. Anyone not caught up in the Overstory hysteria is left to wonder just what these exalted values are. Mass ignorance? Militarism and Inquisitions? Witch burning, anti-Semitism and slavery? By looking at the 100 Mile Christian Walk it is reasonable to conclude that, by and large, the history of Christianity has been a grim enterprise.

A HISTORY OF DISTORTION

Because fundamentalist Christianity is in part driven by historical conclusions pointing to impending calamity, its historical outlook must be carefully examined. In addition to the false impression that Christianity has had a net positive influence on human affairs, I have identified four other false historical impressions generally promoted by today's religious right:

False Impression One: The Jews Have Always Worshipped One God

Acceptance of the myth that human history started at the beginning of the Book of Genesis has until the past few centuries limited inquiry into the origins of modern ideas about God. Scholarly progress over the past 150 years now provides broad insight into the "One True God" of the Jews.

The tribes and nations of the Middle East shared a common mythology 3000 years ago. Versions of similar characters and stories overlap broadly. In the specific case of the ancient Jews, not one God but two are blended in the Bible's Book of Genesis. One account which was written about 950 is centered around Yahweh. A separate writing from about 100 years later (taken from an earlier oral mythology) tells of a god calling himself Elohim. By 750 BCE the two accounts were blended into one, although Genesis as we know it was not completed in its present form until well after 600 BCE. By that time the God of the Jews was understood to be the frequently angry and jealous Yahweh.

Not only was the Hebrew God a combination of more than one god, for much of early Jewish history several gods were accepted and sometimes worshipped at the same time. In addition to Yahweh, who due to his anger was especially popular during times of war, fertility gods like Baal and goddesses such as Asherah were embraced as the Hebrew lifestyle shifted from a nomadic to an agricultural one. It is not a coincidence that Old Testament lore shows Jews worshipping Baal as well as Yahweh.

In order of time, the first false historical assumption of modern Christian fundamentalists is that the God worshipped by the Jews was in place from the beginning of time. Quite the contrary, this God was the product of a Jewish cultural evolution which was never mention during my Calvary Chapel experience.

False Impression Two:
The Leaders of the Reformation Were Enlightened Men

The modern American fundamentalist movement has much in common with the men who began the Protestant Reformation. Like the leaders of today's religious right, Martin Luther and John Calvin were closed-minded religious bigots determined to force their Bible views on all within their reach.

When Luther began the Reformation in 1517, he left Catholicism due to Church wealth and decadence. Luther's movement was welcomed by Northern Europeans who had long resented the Catholic Church's economic and political power. The Protestant separation from Rome did not, however, mark the start of religious freedom or an end to spiritual bigotry. Martin Luther was strongly anti-Semitic and believed that Jews should be deported from Christian countries. He also held dim views of human sexuality, women in general and common people.

As important as Luther has been to the last 500 years of Christian history, his contribution was not as great as that of John Calvin. Calvinism, among other things, provided the framework for the self-righteous "chosen nation" fundamentalism embraced by today's American religious right. Calvin, like Luther, did not believe that God had created all people equal and led a repressive police state in Geneva. Among his more notable deeds was the execution by fire of an enlightened physician, Michael Servetus, due to their differences in Bible interpretation. Not only did Calvin's movement provide the roots of the Baptist movement, it also spawned the witch-burning Puritans.

The intolerant fathers of the Reformation are the direct ideological ancestors of today's religious right. Oddly, John Calvin did not take the entire Bible as literal truth. He viewed much of the Old Testament as lessons God shared with humanity through simple stories. Calvin saw the creation account in Genesis, for example, as God's baby talk given to the common people to inspire their faith.

False Impression Three:
The U.S. Founding Fathers Were "Born Again Christians"

There is no denying that America has always provided a home to more than its share of religious kooks. At the formation of the United States, as is the case today, some members of the Christian lunatic fringe found their way into politics. This having been said, the notion promoted by modern fundamentalists that our nation was founded by "born-again Christians" is an ignorant fallacy at best. On the whole, the Founding Fathers were in favor of strong protection against the intolerant Christian fringe of their own time. The Salem Witch Trials took place only 84 years before the signing of the Declaration of Independence. The creators of our government were understandably mistrustful of people with narrow and closed-minded religious agendas.

The First Amendment to the U.S. Constitution pointedly states that "Congress shall make no law respecting the establishment of religion." While the enlightened leaders of our new nation recognized the utility of the Bible and the various churches, the brightest among them were not in any sense born-again Christians as the term is used today. In fact, the opposite is closer to the truth. Consider the views of the greatest leaders of our nation's founding:

George Washington: Our first President wrote that he was "no bigot to any style of worship" and did not care if those immigrating to the United States were "Mohammedans, Jews, atheists or Christians of any sect" so long as they were good workers.

Benjamin Franklin: This inventor and one of the principal framers of the Declaration of Independence was skeptical of many Christian doctrines and stated "I have some doubts about his (Jesus') Divinity....and think it needless to busy myself with it now."

John Adams: The second American President wrote that he hoped that "translations of the Bible into all languages....will produce translations into English....of the sacred books of the Persians, the Chinese, the Hindus, etc. Then our grandchildren and my great-grandchildren may compare notes and hold fast that all is good."

Thomas Jefferson: America's third President and the principal author of the Declaration of Independence found so much of the Bible distasteful that he edited his own, calling it "The Life and Morals of Jesus of Nazareth." Jefferson's Bible left out the entire Old Testament, all of Paul's letters and the bizarre Book of Revelation. He also blended all four Gospels into one account which omitted Jesus' resurrection.

To be sure, these Founding Fathers were nominal Christians respectful of the value of Christianity in the promotion of social order and stability. Nevertheless, when today's fundamentalists harness the memory of these men to promote their own agenda of spiritual bigotry it is nothing more than a twisted farce.

False Impression Four:
Today's Fundamentalists are Like First Century Christians

Modern fundamentalists have done a clever job of distancing their faith from whatever ugliness they are willing to admit has occurred in Christianity's past. Frequently, those in today's Jesus Movement claim a deep kinship to the small and simple Christian groups of the first century. To say that this is a stretch of the truth is an understatement of the first order. The writings which are now included in the Bible were not listed until 367 CE, so there was no Bible as we know it to study during the first century. This is not to mention that these faithful were generally poor, illiterate and estranged from Imperial Rome, the great military and political power of the day. Today's American fundamentalists frequently pack a "God, guts and guns make America great" mentality into their SUVs for their weekly Bible studies and church services.

Not long ago, I was driving on the freeway when a Ford Expedition adorned with Christian slogans caught my eye. There were two stickers in particular: "Christianity is not a religion-it's a relationship" and "Calvary Chapel- Simply Jesus." Based on what I now know, fundamentalist Christianity certainly is a relationship-with teachers of false history. As for any relationship with the Jesus who actually existed the Overstory is again very far off base.

CHAPTER 2
WHO WAS THAT GUY?

Beyond Contrived Biography

I heard a lot about Jesus during my three years at Mission Valley Christian Fellowship. Jesus' ability to issue every believer a ticket to eternal paradise was endlessly and enthusiastically shared. He was praised as King of kings, most high redeemer and personal savior by those arriving every Sunday in vehicles spreading the word via decal and bumper sticker. In among the fish labeled "truth" devouring fish with legs bearing the inscription "Darwin" was the ever-popular "It's all about Jesus." Perhaps it was, but it wasn't about a Jesus his actual contemporaries would ever have recognized.

In spite of all the Jesus hoopla offered at Mission Valley Christian Fellowship, I do not recall much curiosity about his humanity per se. Did Jesus tell jokes? Did he have a low voice or a squeaky one? Did he sing well? Was he tall or short? While none of these questions are answered in the Bible, what is there does lead to conclusions very different from those offered by the Overstory. Looking back, once I became a regular at my church's Bible studies all of my curiosity about the Jesus of actual history was gone. It was replaced by a desire to gain the favor of those who were leading the Bible studies and the Jesus they described.

Fundamentalist Christians frequently pose the question "Do you believe in Jesus?" What is really being asked is "do you accept our ideas about Jesus?" I now reject the spin put on the central figure of the Overstory by the so-called Jesus Movement, and investigation of the following questions has led me to reasonable conclusions (beliefs if you will) about the historical Christ:

1. Based on the Bible, what insight into the life of Jesus is available?

2. Does the Old Testament foretell the historical Jesus?

3. How do the teachings of Jesus compare to the fundamentalist agenda?

4. Is it possible that Jesus never existed at all?

5. What are the most reasonable conclusions about the life of Jesus?

A BIBLE-BASED BIOGRAPHY

I have reduced what is printed in the Bible about Jesus into twenty-seven entries, in the rough order of their occurrence. While the gospels are frequently not in sync and at times contradict one another, a picture still emerges. What is revealed clearly challenges the fundamentalist Christian Overstory.

One: A Pre-Natal Visit

An unmarried and pregnant Mary visits her cousin Elizabeth who is also expecting a child. Elizabeth's unborn son, who will later be known as John the Baptist, leaps with joy when he recognizes the unborn Jesus in Mary's womb. Elizabeth is filled with the Holy Spirit and shouts to her cousin "blessed are you among women and blessed is the fruit of your womb! (Luke 1:5- 42)."

Two: The Birth of Jesus

Joseph takes the expectant Mary, now his wife, to Bethlehem to comply with a census ordered by Roman Emperor Augustus Caesar. Jesus is born in a manger because there is no room at the local inn. An angel then appears to local shepherds and tells them where to find the newborn Savior (Luke 2:1-12).

Meanwhile, wise men from the east follow a star to Jerusalem and ask King Herod where they can find the newborn King of the Jews. Herod assembles a panel of priests and scribes who determine that the child has been born in Bethlehem. The wise men go there, worshipping the baby Jesus and leaving gifts (Matthew 2:1-11).

Three: The Flight to Egypt

The wise men double-cross Herod and leave Bethlehem without sending word where Jesus can be found. Enraged, Herod orders the execution of all male children two years of age and under in greater Bethlehem. An angel tells Joseph in a dream to take his family to safety in Egypt. After Herod dies, Joseph's family returns to Roman Palestine and settles in Nazareth (Matthew 2:13- 23).

Four: Amazing the Temple Scholars

On a trip to Jerusalem for Passover, Joseph and Mary start back for Nazareth thinking that Jesus is with friends in their local caravan. When they discover that he is missing, the couple frantically returns to Jerusalem. They find the twelve year old Jesus at the temple listening to scholars and asking them incredible questions. When Joseph and Mary chastise their son for his actions, he informs them that he "must be about his Father's business," but they do not understand what he means (Luke 2:41-50).

Five: Jesus is Baptized

John the Baptist is preaching and baptizing sinners in the Jordan River, telling all who will listen of a mighty man who will come to baptize with the Holy Spirit instead of water. Jesus appears and is baptized, after which the Holy Spirit appears as a dove and a voice from heaven shouts out "You are my beloved Son, in whom I am well pleased (Matthew 3:13-17; Mark 1:1-11; Luke 3:21-22)."

Six: Temptation From Satan

Immediately after his baptism Jesus is driven by the Holy Spirit into the wilderness. He fasts for forty days while Satan tempts him with worldly wealth and power. Jesus refuses and the devil departs (Matthew 4:1-11; Mark 1:12-13; Luke 4:1-13).

Seven: A Doubting John The Baptist

Jesus' ministry is gaining momentum. By this time the twelve disciples are in place as is the practice of performing miracles. Nevertheless, two confounding episodes with disciples of John the Baptist take place. First, they criticize Jesus and his inner circle for failing to fast and offer prayers. Later, they are sent by the Baptist himself to ask Jesus if he is really the Messiah (Matthew 9:14; Luke 6:13-16, 7:19-20; John 5:1-9).

Eight: An Uncomfortable Family Moment

While Jesus addresses a large gathering his mother and brothers arrive and ask to speak with him. When he becomes aware of his family's presence, Jesus stretches his hands out toward the disciples and says "here are my mother and my brothers (Mark 3:31-34)."

Nine: A Public Power Failure

Jesus preaches at his hometown synagogue in Nazareth. His neighbors are offended that a member of their community would have the nerve to claim any sort of special wisdom. Jesus finds himself unable to do many miracles because of their disbelief (Mark 6:1-5).

Ten: Deputy Miracle Workers

Jesus gathers his twelve disciples and gives them authority over all demons and the power to heal the sick. They then go and cast out a number of demons and cure many people who have fallen ill (Mark 6:7-13).

Eleven: Exit John the Baptist

Herod Antipas, the ruler of Roman Palestine, has John the Baptist beheaded at the insistence of his sister-in-law. After John's disciples take his torso and bury it in a tomb, some of them insist that their leader has risen from the dead (Mark 6:14-29, Luke 9:7).

Twelve: The Feeding of the Five Thousand

Jesus addresses a crowd of five thousand men and an undetermined number of women and children on a mountain near the Sea of Galilee. As evening approaches Jesus blesses two fish and five loaves of bread. This amount of food is then able to feed the entire crowd with leftovers to spare (John 6:1-13).

Thirteen: After the First Mass Meal

Jesus walks on water in front of his disciples. The next day a group of people from Tiberius ask Jesus to show them a sign and feed them bread from heaven. Jesus refuses, and tells them that he himself is the bread of life. This angers Jewish leaders and leads to the defection of many of his own disciples (John 6:16-66).

Fourteen: Feeding Four Thousand More

In a reprise of the feeding of the five thousand, Jesus feeds four thousand men and uncounted women and children. This time the deed is accomplished with seven loaves of bread and a few little fish (Matthew 15:32-38).

Fifteen: Again No Encore

On the heels of the second miraculous mass-feeding, the Pharisees come to Jesus and demand that he produce a sign from heaven. Jesus refuses, and insults them for asking in the first place (Matthew 16:1-4).

Sixteen: Peter Catches On

Jesus asks his disciples who the people say that he is. They mention John the Baptist as well as reincarnations of the prophets Jeremiah and Elijah. Peter suddenly blurts out "You are the Christ, the Son of the Living God." Jesus then calls Peter the rock on which he will build his church. Jesus also warns the group to keep the fact that he is the Messiah a secret (Matthew 16:13- 20).

Seventeen: A Supernatural Summit

Jesus, Peter, James and John travel to a high mountain where Jesus is transfigured and shines as brightly as the sun. Moses and the prophet Elijah appear and confer with Jesus and a voice from a cloud is heard saying "This is my Son with whom I am well pleased (Matthew 7:1-5)."

Eighteen: Lazarus Rises From the Dead

Jesus visits the Judean town of Bethany and stops by the tomb of

Lazarus who has been dead for four days. He tells a group of by-standers to remove a stone at the tomb's entrance. After they do, Lazarus emerges alive (John 11:5-44).

Nineteen: Jesus Enters Jerusalem

Jesus mounts a colt and enters Jerusalem. A large and excited crowd greets Jesus with palm branches and garments strewn along the road. They are celebrating the arrival of Jesus as the son of David (Matthew 21:7-9; John 12:14-17).

Twenty: The Clearing of the Temple

After entering the temple in Jerusalem, Jesus angrily overturns the tables of the merchants and moneychangers conducting business there. He tells them that they have turned his house into a den of thieves (Mark 11:15-17).

Twenty-One: Judas Cuts a Deal

Satan enters one of Jesus' twelve disciples known as Judas Iscariot. Judas then goes to the ruling priests and accepts an offer of 30 pieces of silver for the deliverance of Jesus into their custody (Matthew 26:14-15; Luke 22:3-5).

Twenty-Two: The Last Supper

Jesus passes out bread and wine. He shares an awareness of his betrayal without naming the culprit. He also specifically predicts Peter's upcoming denial of their association (Mark 14:18- 30).

Twenty-Three: Arrest and Trials

Judas leads a group of soldiers and officials to a garden at a place called Gethsemane. Jesus is then arrested while his disciples flee. He is interrogated, tried, beaten, mocked and dressed in an elegant robe for sentencing by Roman governor Pontius Pilate (Matthew 26:47-56; Luke 22:54- 71, 23:1-12; John 18:1-6).

Twenty-Four: Jesus is Crucified

Pilate finds Jesus innocent of serious wrongdoing and orders a mere flogging. Later, observing a custom of releasing one prisoner to the people at Passover, Pilate asks the gathered crowd if they would like to have Jesus set free. The crowd insists upon the release of a bandit named Barabbas instead. Jesus is nailed to a cross with two common criminals at 9am. Later in the day, darkness envelopes the entire land from noon until three pm (Matthew 27:15-50; Mark 15:6-37; Luke 23:13-46; John 19:1-30).

Twenty-Five: Rise and Shine

After his death on Friday afternoon Jesus is placed in a tomb with a boulder sealing the entrance. The Pharisees request that Pontius Pilate send soldiers to guard the tomb because they fear that Jesus' disciples will steal his body and claim he has risen from the dead. When Mary Magdalene and several other people go to the tomb on Sunday morning an earthquake causes the soldiers to collapse like dead men. Jesus' body is gone and an angel tells the visitors that Jesus has risen (Matthew 27:57-66; Mark 15:42-47; Luke 23:50-56, 24:1-8; John 19:38-42, 20:1).

Twenty-Six: Everybody's Doing It

At the moment Jesus dies an earthquake splits rocks and opens many graves. When Jesus rises from the dead the newly-resurrected group walks into Jerusalem and interacts with the people (Matthew 27:50-53).

Twenty-Seven: A Long Farewell

The tomb guards regain consciousness and report to the chief priests. The priests bribe them to claim that Jesus' body was stolen by the disciples. Undaunted, the risen Jesus appears to some five hundred people over a forty day period following his resurrection. Nearly seven weeks after the crucifixion, Jesus is taken into the sky in front of his disciples (Matthew 28:9-20; Mark 16:14-15; Luke 24:36-53; John 20:13-29, 21:1-14; Acts 1:1-9; I Corinthians 15:3-6).

A SUMMARY OF THE BIBLICAL JESUS

From the vantage point of the Overstory-intoxicated fundamentalist it is a mystery why the nonbeliever cannot "see the truth about Jesus." But, based strictly on the gospels themselves, who he was at any given time is often anything but clear. In three different and crucial areas Jesus frequently appears erratic and evasive:

Identity

After a birth publicly befitting a god-child (entries 1 and 2, above) Jesus is whisked away to Egypt to avoid execution by Herod, who is jealous of the infant's extraordinary nature (entry 3). By the time Jesus is twelve, however, his parents are unable to understand what their son means by saying that he "must be about his fathers business (entry 4)." During his adult ministry the people of his hometown are insulted that Jesus presents himself as anyone special at all (entry 9). He sometimes tells his disciples to keep his identity a secret (entry 16), but the events surrounding his birth would indicate that he was openly a god-man from the very beginning.

Personal Relationships

The Bible reports Jesus in several baffling personal situations. Jesus is disrespectful to his family (entry 8), including his mother who has already been identified as "blessed among women (entry 1)." His disciples are frequently confused about the nature of the man they have dedicated their lives to (entry 16). Perhaps most troubling is the behavior of John the Baptist who, despite having been able to recognize Jesus in the womb (entry 1), expresses critical doubt after the two men have grown to adulthood (entry 7).

Miraculous Abilities

Another confusing area is the on-again, off-again nature of Jesus' miraculous public abilities. Sometime he can't perform miracles (entry 9), and sometimes he refuses to (entries 13 and 15). At the other end of the spectrum is his occasional willingness to show his special talents in front of vast crowds (entries 12 and 14).

The Overstory overemphasizes certain biblical "truths" about Jesus at the clear expense of others. During my Calvary Chapel period I often heard statements like "the Bible tells us that Jesus performed miracles and rose from the dead." But I never heard "the Bible tells us that Jesus was one of at least 13 publicly successful miracle workers during his time. He was also one of a large group of people who resurrected from the dead during that period." The latter statement is equally accurate and much richer in detail.

THE OLD TESTAMENT AND THE HISTORICAL JESUS

Fundamentalists often point to certain details about Jesus included in the New Testament gospels as examples of already fulfilled Old Testament prophecy. The following five examples give reason to suspect that they were either fabricated well after Jesus was executed (the virgin birth, for instance) or were true historical events later assigned Old Testament explanations in order to prop up the case for Jesus as Jewish Messiah (like the clearing of the Jerusalem temple). They are:

The Virgin Birth

The virgin birth reported by Matthew and Luke has been linked to Isaiah 7:14 which says "Behold the virgin shall conceive and bear a Son." Modern scholars point out that virgin birth myths were common in ancient paganism, including the story of Hercules who was born to Alcmene as son of the Greek god Zeus. Also important is the fact that the Hebrew word "almah" as used in Isaiah does not translate as "virgin" but rather as "young woman."

Birth in Bethlehem

First century Jews familiar with Micah 5:2 would not have accepted a Messiah born anywhere other than Bethlehem, the birthplace of King David. Though Jesus grew up in Nazareth, the Gospel of Luke places Joseph's family in Bethlehem at the time of Jesus' birth due to a Roman government census. While conceivable, this explanation finds no support in the other three New Testament gospels. In fact, Mark makes no mention of Bethlehem whatever. Neither does Paul in any of his New Testament writings.

Herod's Infanticide and the Flight to Egypt

The Gospel of Matthew weaves a dramatic tale of an angel's warning to Joseph to "take the young Child and His mother...to Egypt...for Herod will seek the young Child to destroy Him (Matthew 2:13)." This is held up as conformation of Hosea 11.1 which reads "out of Egypt I call my Son." Matthew's account of Herod's killing of all male children two years old and under in and around Bethlehem (Matthew 2:16) finds no support in secular history or any of the other gospels despite it's shocking brutality.

John the Messenger

The imposing figure of John the Baptist had to be accommodated by the gospel writers somehow. Matthew 3:3 explains him as "he who was spoken of by the prophet Isaiah." Isaiah 40.3 tells of "the voice of one crying in the wilderness (saying) 'prepare the way of the Lord.'" What an odd messenger- John baptizes Jesus, then maintains his own set of disciples and sends them to ask Jesus if he is the Messiah in the first place (Luke 7:20).

The Clearing of the Temple

Many objective historians point to Jesus' angry episode at the Jerusalem temple (Matthew 21.12) as the likely reason for his political execution. While Matthew, Mark and Luke place the incident at the end of Jesus' life, John puts it toward the beginning of Jesus' ministry (John 2:14-16), perhaps to cloud the cause and effect relationship between this incident and the crucifixion. The matter has been said to fulfill the very generic Malachi 3:1 which states "the Lord, whom you seek, will suddenly come to His temple."

THE PHILOSOPHY OF JESUS VERSUS THE OVERSTORY

Never is the illogically hypnotic power of the fundamentalist Overstory more obvious than when it is placed against the actual teachings of Jesus of Nazareth. Consider the following:

Jesus was a Pacifist

The anger and militarism associated with the religious right relies upon an Overstory which rides roughshod over the specific teachings of Jesus. The Bible quotes the Nazarene as having said "Blessed are the meek, for they shall inherit the earth (Matthew 5:5)," "Blessed are the peacemakers for they shall be called the sons of God (Matthew 5:9)," and "Love your enemies, bless those who curse you, do good to those who hate you (Matthew 5:44)."

Jesus Was an Activist for the Poor

The corporate greed associated with the right-wing politics embraced by a vast number of today's Christian fundamentalists would surely offend the man who said "Sell whatever you have and give it to the poor (Mark 10:21)," and "Give to everyone who asks of you. And to him who takes away your goods, do not ask for them back (Luke 16:30)."

Jesus Rejected Materialism

The many fundamentalists who view material wealth as "a blessing from the Lord" should double check the words of those to whom they give credit. Jesus is on record as having said "It is easier for a camel to go though the eye of a needle than for a rich man to enter the Kingdom of God (Matthew 19:24)," and "Woe to you who are rich (Luke 6:24)."

Jesus Shunned The Political Establishment

While Jesus was at best indifferent to the political powers of his day, adherents to the Overstory generally embrace a narrow-minded, right-wing agenda and a relentless political activism from the local school board level up. The late author Sinclair Lewis once said "when fascism comes to America it will be wrapped in the flag, carrying a cross." Perhaps prophetically, Sinclair Lewis was right.

THE POSSIBILITY THAT JESUS NEVER EXISTED

The idea that Jesus of Nazareth never existed as a flesh and blood historical figure was more popular among scholars in the late nineteenth and early twentieth centuries than it is today. Nevertheless, it is enough of a possibility to be mentioned here despite the fact that I do not personally subscribe to the theory. Some interesting food for thought:

An Absence in Roman History

There is great historical drama present in the gospels, including three hours of midday darkness supposedly witnessed by Jew and Roman alike (Matthew 27:45). The Romans kept meticulous historical records and left no mention of the life, activities, trial or execution of Jesus of Nazareth. It is not until the year 117 CE that Christians find their way into Roman records, when Tacitus mentions problems the new religion was causing.

No Presence in Contemporary Jewish Writings

Philo was a prolific Jewish author from the time Jesus is said to have lived and ministered. While Philo leaves an extensive account of Pontius Pilate, he makes no mention of Jesus whatever. Justin of Tiberius, also a Jew from Jesus' time and place, left a history covering the period from Moses to the mid-first century. Again, not a word concerning Jesus.

Flavius Josephus, a Jew and Roman Citizen, was a widely-respected first century historian. He appears to have left an account of Jesus in his classic "Antiquities of the Jews." His apparent description of Jesus as "a miracle worker," and "the Messiah" have been used by Christians as independent verification of the gospel accounts. Modern scholarship, however, has shown these passages to be frauds which were added by the early Catholic Church. There are obvious differences in style between the passages concerning Jesus and the rest of the book. Josephus also produced a legitimate account of John the Baptist which makes no mention of Jesus at all.

The Talmud, a record of Jewish oral law and history which was written around 200 CE, does mention one Yeshu the Nazarene. Since the name translates into "Jesus" in Greek and Jesus was known as a Nazarene, this may serve as some independent historical verification. If it does, it also provides some pointed contradictions of the gospels. Yeshu had only five disciples named Mattai, Nakkia, Netzer, Buni and Todah. He was executed by hanging on the eve of Passover for sorcery and having a bad influence on Israel.

Irreconcilable Gospel Contradictions

The gospel accounts of Matthew and Luke present detailed genealogies of Jesus. Each attempts to present him as a descendant of King David. The two accounts could hardly agree less with each other. In addition to contradictory information about Jesus' connection to David, an historical impossibility arises: Matthew reports the virgin birth during the reign of King Herod who died in 4 BCE while Luke places the same event at the time of the census of Quirinius, which took place in 6 CE.

CONCLUSIONS ABOUT THE HISTORICAL JESUS

The gospels at times present a rough outline of the career and teachings of Jesus of Nazareth. Some of the unflattering episodes admitted to by the gospel writers point to a high likelihood that he actually existed. Placing these reports against a backdrop of verifiable history has allowed for the following conclusions:

Jesus' Birth

Jesus was probably born in the final years of the reign of King Herod, likely around 5 BCE. The birth more likely took place in Nazareth than in Bethlehem, as the latter location makes no sense other than as an attempt to harmonize the event with Old Testament prophecy. Matthew is consistent about the birth occurring while Herod (who died in 4 BCE) was still alive. Luke promotes a Bethlehem birthplace by linking it to the 6 CE census of Quirinius, then overrules this likely fabrication by also asserting that it happened "in the days of Herod (Luke 1:5)."

Childhood, Youth and Education

Jesus grew up in obscurity in Nazareth. Save for one mention by Luke of an event when he was twelve (Luke 2:42-50), there are no accounts of Jesus' youth in the four gospels. In later accounts of his adulthood, Jesus was said to have been the son of a carpenter (Matthew 13:55) and a carpenter in his own right (Mark 6:3). He was not from the class of people who would have received training in Hebrew, and almost certainly spoke Aramaic. The scriptures indicate that he was at least marginally literate (Luke 4:16-20), but curiously left no writings of his own.

Ministry

Jesus began as a follower of John the Baptist and was baptized by his mentor prior to undertaking a separate ministry. His ministry could have been as short as one year, as Mark's gospel would indicate, or as long as the three years pointed to by the Gospel of John.

Political Execution

Mark's account of the clearing of the Jerusalem temple as the catalyst for Jesus' execution is likely. While some hand may have been played by Jewish religious leadership, Roman Procurator Pontius Pilate was responsible for the crucifixion. By the time Mark wrote the Bible's first gospel it was important to excuse the Romans from blame. They had destroyed Jerusalem in 70 CE and it would have served no purpose to rile them up by the time Mark's gospel was written around the year 75.

Events Following the Death of Jesus

A claim that Jesus rose from the dead, just like one which had been circulated earlier about John the Baptist (Luke 9:7), was anticipated by both the Pharisees and the Roman authorities (Matthew 27:64-66). The gospels disagree about what happened after the reported resurrection, with Matthew and Mark reporting posthumous appearances only around Galilee. Luke reports these occurrences exclusively in the Jerusalem area.

The most consistent presence around the rumored resurrection is that of Mary Magdalene. All speculation about the true nature of her relationship with Jesus aside, there is a good chance that she told Peter that Jesus had resurrected spiritually, rather than physically. The Bible itself reports that Jesus "appeared in another form (Mark 16:7-12)."

Conclusion

It is some two thousand years since the time of Jesus. The best evidence shows us that Jesus of Nazareth was the leader of a religious group during a time when many would-be Messiahs were active in Roman Palestine. He was not the best known of them- that distinction belonged to John the Baptist. The Bible tells us that Jesus lived in a place and time where miracles and rising from the dead were fairly common occurrences and not limited to him. One thing, however, remains clear: the historical Jesus was an enlightened man with a compelling message. Whether or not one considers him to be God, or to have been a god, is another matter altogether.

CHAPTER 3
THE WRONG GOD

Beyond Limiting The Limitless

"Do you believe in God?" Perhaps no imaginable question assumes more. This question also gives those who are selling the fundamentalist Overstory a huge advantage over any potential recruit. What is really being asked is "do you accept my concept of God?" Our common cultural background has forged a rough outline of what this deity might be like and leaves even nonbelievers somewhat familiar with the God of the Christian fundamentalist. What is left is a decision to accept or reject the icon of the Overstory.

Before any decision is ever made about anything, it is best to understand the nature of what is being discussed in the first place. Never is Overstory doublespeak more obvious than when broad, objective questions are asked about the nature of the God they claim to have specific answers about. The following clear and simple questions, when posed to a recruiting Christian fundamentalist, will yield anything but clear and simple answers:

FOUR ESSENTIAL QUESTIONS CONCERNING GOD

Is God Infinite?

The late Chuck Chamberlain may have said it best when he noted that "if there was anything other than God, God would not be infinite, He would be finite." While the few fundamentalists I had occasion to ask indicated that their God is infinite, the Overstory hammers home a contradictory mantra of "worship the creator, not his creation." If the creation is not God, then God is finite- limited by everything that he is not.

Is God All Powerful?

Not long ago a fundamentalist acquaintance told me of being tested by Satan. I pointed out that if God has powers opposing him, he could not be all powerful. She responded that God is all powerful but that the rest of us, including Satan, have been given free will to use the power of our thoughts and actions to oppose him. Her explanation, the standard fundamentalist line on the matter, still leaves the Overstory God without all power. Her response did not explain how God is all powerful but rather illuminated, within the fundamentalist framework, why he is not!

Is God All Knowing?

The God of the Bible, if that source is to be taken literally, shows himself to know far less than everything. A clear illustration of this can be found is in the tale of Sodom and Gomorrah. Genesis 18:20-21 quotes God as follows: "because the outcry against Sodom and Gomorrah is great...I will go down now and see whether they have done altogether according to the outcry against it that has come to Me; and if not, I will know."

This same God is also capable of second guessing himself when circumstances fail to meet his expectations. In the buildup to the story of Noah and the Great Flood (Genesis 6:5-6), the reader encounters this: "the Lord saw that the wickedness of man was great in the earth...And the Lord was sorry that He had made man on the earth." Would an all-knowing God not be aware of what to expect in the first place?

Is God a Good Parent?

The God of the Overstory is a male parent who is said to love humanity while wanting more than anything to receive this love in return. But, the fundamentalists tell us, he will not force anyone to love him- each individual's free will must render a decision to accept or reject the love of this eternal father. During my Calvary Chapel period I accepted this explanation quietly enough. In the ensuing years, however, this illustration has shown itself to be utterly ridiculous for a number of reasons.

Consider the quality of the parenting we are faced with in the Overstory. A father who knows everything should not let his weak and ignorant children make a decision between heaven and hell while giving invisible evil forces free reign to tempt them. Satan and his demons are allowed to act relentlessly against his children's eternal welfare. And how does our father decide to protect his besieged offspring? By leaving them a collection of writings (the Bible), many of which are impossible for reasonable people to accept as literal truth. Adding insult to injury are the frequently obnoxious spokespeople claiming to be explaining God for God.

Think about it- a parent knowing better than his children, and knowing that he knows better, should not leave the choice between eternal bliss and eternal torture in his children's inadequate hands. If such a heavenly father indeed exists I sincerely hope there is a cosmic Child Protection Bureau planning to visit him with some hard questions in the very near future!

JOSH MC DOWELL'S LOGIC TRAP

Whatever qualities God may or may not actually possess, the Overstory tells us that sinful nonbelievers are separated from their God and that he is blameless in the matter. We sinners, so the story goes, have only one method by which to regain God's favor: through a "personal relationship with Jesus Christ." Why is this? Because this heavenly father loves us and appeared on earth as Jesus some 2000 years ago, was executed in his human body and then came back from the dead. This sacrifice was necessary, it is said, because it allows God to substitute the torture and crucifixion of Jesus as ransom for our individual sins. This is confusingly convoluted because Jesus is said to be God in the first place.

How one can be certain that Jesus Christ (whoever he really was) was truly God (whatever that actually is) has been explained for fundamentalist recruiters by author Josh McDowell. His popular book "Evidence That Demands a Verdict" argues that a man who claims to be God could only fall into one of the following three categories: Liar, Lunatic or Lord. Objective research has convinced me that, whatever he was claiming, the historical Jesus did not understood the concept of God in a manner which resembles the beliefs of the modern American religious right. Nevertheless, we will examine McDowell's outline on God as Jesus of Nazareth using the author's own parameters.

Was Jesus a Liar?

The Fundamentalist Outlook: He Wouldn't Have Died for a Lie

McDowell shares the opinion that if Jesus wasn't God he was a liar and a fool for making such a claim in the first place because it lead to his execution. A liar would have admitted he was lying before it cost him his life.

What Fundamentalists Overlook:
Jesus Was Not Executed for Claiming He Was God

As we saw in the previous chapter, Jesus wasn't executed for claiming he was God. The best historical evidence shows that he was executed for political reasons. The situation came to a head when he violently cleared the Jewish temple in Jerusalem.

Was Jesus Insane?

The Fundamentalist Outlook: It is Absurd to Suggest That Jesus Was Insane

Proponents of the Overstory point to the content of Jesus' teachings to quickly dismiss any questions about his mental health.

What Fundamentalists Overlook: Some Who Knew Jesus Thought Him Insane

The Bible shows us that Jesus' sanity was certainly not beyond question, even among those who knew him well. Following an intense episode of healing and demon confrontation Mark 3:21 tells us: "when His own people heard about this, they went out to lay hold of Him, for they said 'He is out of His mind.'"

Was Jesus God?

The Fundamentalist Outlook: He Was God, and That Made Him Different

The Overstory tells us that Jesus was God and that every other human being in history was, or is, not. He was perfect and flawless, the rest of us shameful and defective to the extent that his grim and sadistic fate was somehow necessary.

What Fundamentalists Overlook: If God is Infinite, We Are All Part of God

Again, you cannot have an infinite God and anything other than God. Jesus was not special due to a nature different from the rest of humanity, but due to the depth of his understanding. He was an enlightened being who fully recognized his true nature when those around him had not yet developed that ability.

FUNDAMENTALISTS: LIARS, LUNATICS OR LIMITED?

Using the following variation of Josh McDowell's misguided logic-trap, an open minded individual will see that Christian fundamentalists fall into three clear categories:

Some Fundamentalists Are Liars

Liars in Leadership

Hypocrisy and deception on the part of the loudest element of fundamentalist Christian leadership has been frequently exposed over the past decades. Among the highest-profile examples: Jim Bakker, co-host of television's PTL (for "Praise the Lord") Club was accused of rape and convicted of financially defrauding many of his followers. Among his critics when the scandal broke in 1987 was Jimmy Swaggart, another very public fundamentalist media-mouthpiece. At that time Swaggart called Bakker a "cancer on the body of Christ" on Larry King's television program. The following year, Jimmy Swaggart was exposed as the customer of a Louisiana prostitute.

More recently Ted Haggard, pastor of the New Life Church of Colorado Springs and a spiritual advisor to President George W. Bush, was forced to resign leadership of the National Association of Evangelicals in November, 2006. The resignation followed the revelation that Haggard had been involved with a male prostitute from whom he had purchased methamphetamine. Haggard appeared in the documentary "Jesus Camp" where he is seen telling the faithful "we don't have to debate what we should think about homosexual activity. It's written in the Bible."

Liars in the Laity

My experience as a member of Mission Valley Christian Fellowship was disappointing for a number of reasons. One of them was that its members did not seem to be any more truthful than any other random group. Gossip, infidelity and scandal seemed to occur with the same regularity as it would anywhere else- this despite lives supposedly changed deeply by Jesus. Perhaps it was simply due to a cocky over-reliance on the popular slogan "Christians aren't perfect- just forgiven."

Liars due to Indoctrination

One of the most frightening fundamentalist characteristics is the confident repetition of falsehoods which are passed from the top down. Statements like "America was founded by born-again Christians" are spread by people who are not aware that they are false in the first place. These lies are passed from teacher to pupil, almost always without any serious effort by either to objectively verify whether or not they are actually true.

Some Fundamentalists are Truly Lunatics

Lunatics in Leadership

Some of fundamentalist Christianity's best known spokesmen have made comments which should sound objectively insane to any rational person. Jerry Falwell, who died in 2007, was the founder of the right-wing Moral Majority political organization as well as a highly successful televangelist. He was responsible for an almost endless list of frighteningly irrational comments. Among them: "the idea that religion and politics don't mix was invented by the devil to keep Christians from running their own country," "good Christians, like slaves and soldiers, ask no questions," and "AIDS is not just God's punishment for homosexuals, it is God's punishment for the society that tolerates homosexuals."

Falwell's friend and fellow televangelist Pat Robertson, founder of the Christian Broadcasting Network and host of an immensely successful television program "The 700 Club," is every bit as detached from objective reality. From a wealth of illustrative Pat Robertson quotes, I chose my personal favorite. During the July 8,

[41]

1997 broadcast of his program, he began to rail against those fasci-
nated with the subject of UFOs and space aliens by saying "can a
demon appear as a slanty-eyed, funny-looking creature? Of course
he can, or it can. Of course they can deceive people. And if they
can lead somebody away from the true God, or away from Jesus
Christ…you will lose your salvation."

Lunatics in the Laity

While it is certainly reasonable to question the sanity of those who
accept the ideas promoted by the likes of Pat Robertson, an ex-
tended discussion of the mental health of fundamentalist church
members would require a book in itself. Summarized very briefly,
modern psychologists note that the goal of mental wholeness is extremely difficult for individuals who see a universe composed of
two mismatching parts- one good and one evil, one visible and one
invisible- which are constantly at odds.

By looking at one individual whose mental illness brought him
wide notoriety, the psychological torture of the fundamentalist
Overstory comes to light. Mark David Chapman, a delusional man
considered by some experts to be psychotic, became a born-again
Christian at the age of 16. His religious activities included the dis-
tribution of Bible tracts as well as comedy and musical perform-
ances at Christian churches and social centers. At the same time
Chapman loved the music of the Beatles, especially John Lennon,
a vocal critic of organized religion. The struggle in Chapman's
mind led to the Lennon's murder on December 8, 1980.

Lunatics by Indoctrination

One of history's most baffling questions concerns the behavior of
average German Christians during the 1930s and 1940s as the Jewish Holocaust unfolded. After Hitler's fall, many surviving Ger-
mans described a gradual mind-numbing due to Nazi propaganda
against the Jews. This concept of mass-insanity by indoctrination

could help explain why modern American Christian fundamentalists support an Overstory promoting materialistic greed and militaristic violence in the name of Jesus, a politically alienated pacifist of very modest means.

All Fundamentalists Are Conceptually Limited

Limited by Upbringing

Fundamentalist parents use the God of the Overstory as the answer to important questions posed by their children. As the child's mind develops, dangerously narrow limits on his or her concept of God develop due to ongoing indoctrination. The idea of a personal relationship with an invisible Superman/Santa Claus figure is in place before a child has developed the ability to reason. By the time he or she can read, the habit of calling on their God's Superman powers for help with problems and Santa Claus side for material favors is well entrenched. Unfortunately and dangerously, so is the notion that those with other religious concepts and traditions merit punishment in an eternal hell.

Limited by Frame of Reference

Adults in our society not raised with, or not accepting, the Overstory often find themselves troubled at some time by their life situations. In response, a spiritual curiosity arises which is eagerly addressed by fundamentalist acquaintances. Since the basic premise of the Jesus Movement is culturally familiar, the Overstory pitch will often feel more comfortable than an open-minded quest for true enlightenment.

Once a new recruit is exposed to the seductive appeal of come-as-you-are Christianity, the search for God ends almost as soon as it started. The troubled seeker becomes a closed-minded convert in the blink of an eye. New fundamentalists can go from knowing little about God to thinking they know everything in a very short time!

[43]

Limited by Indoctrination

Whatever a person's background, an ongoing exposure to the Overstory has an ironic effect. While the church services and Bible studies are said to promote spiritual maturity and discernment, the opposite actually takes place. An infinite God appears petty and limited due to a multi-faceted brainwashing. Ultimately, everyone who finds truth in anything other than the twisted Overstory is deemed deserving of eternal suffering.

To be sure, both garden variety liars and obvious lunatics have had a substantial impact on the creation and promotion of the Overstory. But their contributions pale when compared to the problems caused by fundamentalist limits on the concept of God and the disrespectful comparison of these arbitrary limits to the spiritual paths of all others. God can only peacefully resonate when recognized as limitless and beyond the realm of all comparison. The following examination of the four basic outlooks on God, three limiting and one unifying, will illustrate:

FOUR OUTLOOKS ON THE INFINITE

Atheism: God Is Nothing

Atheism is built on the premise that God is nothing, and nothing is God. If the Overstory provided the only god concept on the face of our planet, the appeal of atheism would be admittedly overwhelming. But thankfully this is not the case, and Western atheism's premise that God is nothing finds its very strength in the shortcomings of literalist Christianity, and particularly Christianity's frequent hostility to empirical science. Rejecting the obvious flaws of fundamentalism in no way proves or disproves the presence of one all powerful and infinite energy.

Polytheism: There Are Many Gods

Quite early in the history of humankind, unseen personalities were created to explain natural phenomena. Eventually, various supernatural beings were prayed to and appeased with rituals. This was the dawn of religion as we know it. By the time Western Civilization appeared, polytheism was well entrenched all around the Mediterranean Sea. The Greeks and Romans shared elaborate tales describing their many gods interacting with each other and with human beings.

By the time of Jesus the sophistication of the classic cultures had spawned dissatisfaction with their polytheistic traditions. Curiosity about the monotheism present in the southern Mediterranean, especially Judaism, arose in places like Rome and Athens. This fascination later helped fuel the spread of early Christianity into Europe. Polytheism today is largely an Eastern phenomenon best illustrated by Hinduism, India's predominant religion.

Monotheism: There Is One God

Some seven centuries before the birth of Jesus of Nazareth the Hebrew people were evolving from a polytheistic culture into one which worshipped only one god known as Yahweh. Roughly six hundred years after Jesus was executed, the prophet Mohammed began the religion known as Islam. Judaism, Christianity and Islam are now called the three great monotheistic religions because all three share a common background and all are said to worship one god. In the case of Christianity, however, it took hundreds of years to fully articulate the three separate personalities of the one god Christians claim to worship.

Enlightened Pantheism: God Is One

As we have seen, if God is indeed infinite and all powerful then pantheism is the only enlightened outlook. Atheism, polytheism and monotheism either fail to recognize spirituality altogether (atheism) or create theological systems which limit the gods they describe (polytheism and monotheism). Pantheism is found in the teachings and practices of Zen Buddhism and Advaita Vedanta, a tradition found in generally polytheistic Hinduism. In the West, those who recognize the unity present in all things are frequently associated with the broad term "New Age Movement." In the darkness of the Overstory, the term is actually used derisively.

Today, humanity finds itself teetering on the edge of self-destruction. This situation is due in no small part to differences between the three major monotheistic traditions- Judaism, Christianity and Islam. Some background on the God-views of these powerful religions is our next order of business.

DIFFERENCES IN "THE ONE TRUE GOD"

The Evolution of the God of the Jews

As we saw in our survey of history, the Hebrew people did not start out as a monotheistic people. It is almost certain that Yahweh, the God of the Jews, evolved over time from the Canaanite deity El, whose name provides the final two letters in the word Israel. El is a broad Semitic word for god, and to the people of Canaan he was the father of the very popular Baal, a dying god who influenced the weather and fertilized the earth. Chapter 17 of Genesis shows God introducing himself to Abraham as "El of the mountain."

Yahweh was endowed with many of the qualities common to gods of the greater Middle East. He controlled the weather, manipulated the seas, and was an angry and jealous war deity. From the standpoint of lasting influence he was most of all judgmental, punishing and prone to meddle in human history. Ironically, those who named Yahweh had an enlightened perspective. Their god's name, written "YHWY," was derived from the verb "to be" and Yahweh tells Moses in Exodus 3:14 "I am that I am." In other words, whoever wrote these words down was aware that God is that which is- the pantheistic outlook!

How Jesus of Nazareth Became God

In light of the fact that it took Yahweh many centuries to evolve from his cradle of Middle Eastern mythology, it is not surprising that that the nature of the Christian God was not clearly stated until some 300 years after the time of the Christ. While Jesus is still held to have been the Jewish Messiah, Judaism and Christianity parted ways completely within decades of his crucifixion. This was largely due to the fact that Gentile influence had twisted Jesus' story out of all traditional Jewish context. The anticipated Hebrew Messiah would have been a unique man sent by God, but certainly not God himself.

Had Jesus returned to earth in the very short time he promised the creativity required to forge the Trinity would never have been necessary. After enough time had passed to negate Jesus' guarantee that the world would end within a generation of his own time (Luke 21:32), new concepts came into play. Could Jesus have been God? If so, how could his father also be God and there still be only one God? Many new ideas were debated as Gentile influence, especially Greek, increasingly shaped Christian thought.

As the second century progressed a two-god Christian concept was promoted by Marcion of Sinope. Marcion (100-165 CE) was a theologian and controversial bishop from what is now Northern Turkey. He promoted the idea that the Old Testament God, while creator of the earth, was a cold-hearted tyrant who made unreasonable demands upon humanity. Marcion taught that Jesus of Nazareth was the incarnation of a second god who sought to bring love and liberation to humanity. The god of Jesus asked for only faith and love, while Yahweh demanded adherence to an impossible set of laws.

Marcion's outlook gained a substantial following, due in no small part to the fact that it made sense. The additional influence of Arius (250-336 CE), an elder in the church in Alexandria, fueled further controversy. Arius taught that Jesus was created by his father after the beginning of time and was rewarded with divinity based upon the quality of his life. Those Christians promoting

Yahweh and Jesus as absolute equals had to come up with a plausible explanation.

The anti-Marcion, anti-Arius element came up with so many variations of their one God that Christianity was in a full-blown crisis by the year 300. Fearing a weakening of the Christian faith he had embraced, Roman Emperor Constantine called all bishops to a meeting in Nicea (present- day Turkey) in 325 and ordered them to define the God of their faith. The Trinity as we now know it was then created.

As we saw in the first chapter, the Western understanding of the Trinity God in its present form can be traced to Constantine's Council of Nicea. Jesus and his father were there declared to be "of one substance" in a creed which included "we believe in the Holy Spirit." This concept would not have made sense to Jesus of Nazareth. The founder of Christianity never once alluded to a Trinity. He was declared by men to be part of it long after his time on earth.

The God of Muhammad

Standing in the planet-threatening shadow cast by Islamic and Christian fundamentalists, it is easy to lose sight of the fact that they are similar religions with a common background. The God of the Islamic holy book, the Koran, bears a stunning likeness to the father God present in the Old Testament of the Bible. He is said to be a perfect being who created the entire universe, still sustains his creation, and is the judge of humanity. The Koran is viewed as the final revelation to humanity from a series that started with Abraham and progressed through Moses and Jesus. The message was perfected and completed in God's communications to the prophet Muhammad (570-632 CE) during the early part of the seventh century. The Koran states that Muslims are on "the same course of faith as...Moses, Abraham and Jesus,...and do not differ in it (Surah 42:13)."

Where the Koran takes exception to Jews and Christians is in assuming that God's favor falls upon their specific religions. The Koran states "They say 'none shall ever enter Paradise unless he be a Jew or a Christian.' These are their wishful beliefs...The truth of the matter is, whoever submits himself entirely to Allah (God) and he is a doer of good to others shall have his reward with the Lord (Surah 2:111-112)." In other words, even Islam at its best teaches that it is folly to limit that which has no limits.

The insanity present in Western monotheism becomes glaringly apparent when placed in the context of the twenty-first century. A tragically familiar episode occurred on September 11, 2001 when lunatic Islamic fundamentalists flew jet aircraft into the World Trade Center in New York and the Pentagon in Washington, D.C. The late Reverend Jerry Falwell commented in the aftermath of the grim event as follows: "I really believe that the pagans, and the abortionists, and the feminists, and the gays and the lesbians who are actively trying to make that an alternative lifestyle, the ACLU, People for the American Way, all of them who have tried to secularize America, I point the finger in their face and say you helped this happen...the abortionists have got to bear some of the burden for this because God will not be mocked."

What the likes of Osama bin Laden and Jerry Falwell have never been able to see is the sheer insanity of placing limits on a limitless God. The pressure of trying to force the square peg of fundamentalism, no matter the flavor, into the round hole of an infinite God creates the tension we witness today.

People do not fly planes into buildings because they worship the wrong God. Rather, they terrorize those who are different because they have convinced themselves that others worship the wrong God.

CHAPTER 4
DARKNESS AND ZOMBIES

Beyond Book Idolatry

After I joined Mission Valley Christian Fellowship during the summer of 1995 it quickly became apparent that the answer to everything was in the Bible. I was encouraged to read it and attend studies on a regular basis. Since I was told that it was all about Jesus, I decided to start with the gospel stories at the beginning of the New Testament. By mid-October I had read and studied the first two, Matthew and Mark, in the recommended New King James Bible I still study today.

Near the end of October a neighbor invited me to his upcoming Halloween party. The following Sunday, thinking it was merely small talk, I mentioned the invitation to a fellow worshipper after church. She told me that Halloween glorifies Satan and that a better alternative was available in the October 31 carnival on our church grounds. Not wanting to look like a friend of the devil, I made an excuse to my neighbor and spent Halloween night in the church parking lot eating and playing games.

The church carnival notwithstanding, it occurred to me that I had come across imagery in the Bible harmonious with Halloween. Returning to my New King James I reviewed Matthew 27:45,51-53 which describes the afternoon of Jesus' execution: There was darkness all over the land from noon until three p.m. Then "the earth quaked, and the rocks were split, and the graves were opened, and many bodies of the saints who had fallen asleep were raised; and coming out of the graves after His resurrection, they went into the holy city and appeared to many." This atmosphere of darkness and zombies was amplified by Mark 16:17-18 where Jesus says "In my name they will cast out demons, they will speak with new tongues; they will take up serpents; and if they drink anything deadly it will by no means hurt them." Had I read the Book of Revelation by that time, many more ghoulish images would have been known to me.

Wanting to be a new Christian who knew his way around the Bible, I shared my dark passages with the woman who had warned me about Halloween in the first place. Rather than complimenting my scholarship, she suggested a talk with an associate pastor. Not desiring to risk a negative reaction from the leaders of my new-found reality, I set the matter aside.

It was soon time to prepare for my first born-again Christmas. By December I had completed the gospel of Luke and was reading the final gospel, John. I was surprised to find no Christmas story in John's account of Jesus' life. Reviewing the other three gospels, I also noted that Mark doesn't begin until Jesus is a grown man. Returning to Matthew and Luke I wound up with as many questions as answers because the two accounts are not at all alike. Matthew features wise men following a star and bearing gifts, but makes no mention of a manger. His baby Jesus is found in a Bethlehem house. Luke's tale is centered in a manger, but there are no wise men among his shepherds and angels. The familiar Christmas story turned out to be the best of Matthew and Luke blended into one.

As Easter 1996 approached, I found a new source of concern. I wanted to understand Good Friday before observing it and again went to the Bible to discover some glaring contradictions. What was said on the sign attached to Jesus' cross by Roman soldiers is reported four different ways in the four different gospels. In order of increasing length they appear in the Bible in bold capital letters as follows:

Mark: THE KING OF THE JEWS.

Luke: THIS IS THE KING OF THE JEWS.

Matthew: THIS IS JESUS THE KING OF THE JEWS.

John: JESUS OF NAZARETH, THE KING OF THE JEWS.

The gospel details surrounding the discovery that Jesus was missing from his tomb on Sunday morning are also contradictory. The people present at the tomb, who they encountered and what they found break down as follows:

MARK: Mary Magdalene, Mary the mother of James and Salome enter Jesus' tomb and find a young man in a white robe.

LUKE: Mary Magdalene, Joanna, Mary the mother of James and "the other women with them" discover two men in shining garments in the tomb.

MATTHEW: Mary Magdalene and "the other Mary" are present at the tomb during an earthquake and then an angel comes down from heaven.

JOHN: Mary Magdalene, Peter and another disciple go to Jesus' tomb where Mary meets two angels inside.

I was bothered by the fact that such important and simple details were not recorded without contradiction in the supposedly inerrant word of God. Despite some well-founded fear of disapproval, I shared my concerns with a Bible-savvy friend at church. He grabbed his Bible and read aloud to me from I Corinthians 3:18-20: "Let no one deceive himself. If anyone among you seems to be wise in this age, let him become a fool that he may become wise. For the wisdom of this world is foolishness with God. For it is written 'he catches the wise with their own craftiness' and again 'The Lord knows the thoughts of the wise, that they are futile.'" Not clear-headed enough to mention that my worldly wisdom was nothing more than the Bible quoted verbatim, I accepted my friend's promise that Christian maturity would later allow me an understanding of the Bible in its proper context. To start me on my way he gave me three New Testament quotes to memorize. They were:

1. JOHN 3:3: "Most assuredly, I say unto you, that unless one is born again, he cannot see the Kingdom of God."

2. JOHN 3:16: "For God so loved the world that He gave His only begotten Son, that whoever believes in Him shall not perish but have eternal life."

3. John 14:6: "I am the way, the truth, and the life. No one comes to the Father except through Me."

Equipped with these three key quotes and a variety of church-approved study aids, I read the entire Bible twice in the two years which followed. I apparently grew in spiritual discernment and by the end of this period I was teaching a fourth grade Sunday school class. Gradually however, I developed objections to God's behavior as reported in a number of Bible stories.

The more I studied the Bible, the less sense fundamentalism made to me. My enthusiasm for every aspect of the Overstory had worn thin by the summer of 1998 and I left Mission Valley Christian Fellowship. It had become apparent that while scripture was the final word on everything, its interpretation required a context missing in the writings themselves. I came to see that if the books of the Old and New Testaments were read without being filtered through the Overstory, the Bible could not mean what I had been told it did. Eventually, three new and reasonable alternative contexts occurred to me. They were:

I. God the Sinner Becomes God the Saint

When the Bible is read with even a slightly open mind, it is obvious that the God of the Old Testament suffers from some serious character defects. In this light, the New Testament reports the amends made by an apologetic God in his incarnation as Jesus Christ.

One of the Father's more glaring deficiencies concerns unreasonable jealousy and resentment. Consider Exodus 20:5. The verse reads "I, the Lord your God, am a jealous God, visiting the iniquity of the fathers upon the children to the third and fourth generations of those who hate me." The mental health of a God who is insecure enough to be jealous of human beings aside, it is insanely spiteful to place a curse upon the innocent great-grandchildren of those who have sinned.

God the Father was also irrationally punitive about the human sexuality he designed in the first place. A reading of Leviticus 20:9-18 shows the death penalty as God's required punishment for homosexuality, bestiality, adultery and certain acts of prostitution. Leviticus also mandates a life of exile for couples who engage in sex during the woman's menstrual period.

The cruelty God displays in the Old Testament can be heart rending. In Numbers 15:32-56 a man is caught gathering sticks on the Sabbath. God tells Moses to have his congregation stone the man to death, which they promptly do. The Father also initiated inexcusable violence against enemies of the Jews. Numbers 31:1-18 shows Yahweh telling Moses to burn down all the cities where Midianites had lived. He mandated that the Jews kill all Midianite men, male children and women who were not virgins.

The Jews themselves were by no means spared from Yahweh's mean streak. God's revenge is inflicted upon them in Lamentations 4:4, 9-11 as follows: "The tongue of the infant clings to the roof of its mouth for thirst; The young children ask for bread, but no one breaks it for them…The hands of the compassionate women have cooked their own children; They became food for them in the destruction of the daughter of my people. The Lord has fulfilled His fury, He has poured out His fierce anger. He kindled a fire in Zion, and it has devoured its foundations."

In this sinner-to-saint alternative theology, God gains mental stability and emotional maturity as time passes. When he begins to accept that humanity's suffering is in part due his own shortcomings, God appears on earth as Jesus of Nazareth and lives a life dedicated to kindness, compassion and pacifism. As Jesus, God specifically overrules angry mandates from his past. Regretting earlier unreasonable reactions to human sexuality, Jesus makes amends in an incident recorded in John 8:3-11: "The scribes and the Pharisees brought...a young woman caught in adultery...they said to Him 'Teacher, this woman was caught in adultery, the very act. Now Moses, in the law, commanded us that she should be stoned. But what do you say?'...He raised Himself up and said to them 'He who is without sin among you, let him throw a stone at her first... When Jesus had raised Himself up and saw no one but the woman, He said to her 'Woman where are those accusers of yours? Has no one condemned you?' She said 'No one, Lord.' And Jesus said to her 'Neither do I condemn you.'"

In Mark 2:23-24,27 Jesus pointedly reverses the Old Testament execution of the man who had gathered sticks on the Sabbath. It reads "Now it happened that He (Jesus) went to the grain fields on the Sabbath; and as they went His disciples plucked heads of grain. And the Pharisees said to Him 'Look, why do they do what is not lawful on the Sabbath?'...And He said to them 'The Sabbath was made for man, and not man for the Sabbath.'" At the end of his ministry, according to this alternative theology, Jesus is crucified to atone for sin. But not for the sins of humanity against God but for God's sins against humanity.

II. It's All About the Holy Spirit

In Matthew 12:31-32 Jesus says "every sin and every blasphemy will be forgiven men, but the blasphemy of the Holy Spirit will not be forgiven men. Anyone who speaks a word against the Son of Man, it will be forgiven him, but whoever speaks against the Holy Spirit it will not be forgiven him." In my later days at Mission Valley I asked an associate pastor for an explanation. He told me "don't worry about what that means- just keep your eyes on Jesus and walk the Christian walk and you're good for eternity."

I have taken a deeper look at this passage since leaving the fold, and it has provided my second alternative theology. Jesus' words indicate that the Holy Spirit is in some way superior to God the Son. Otherwise, blasphemy against one would be identical to blasphemy against the other. The key to spiritual freedom lies in understanding why the Holy Spirit is superior to the other two persons of the traditional Trinity.

God the Son is believed to have lived among us for about 33 years roughly 2000 years ago, and fundamentalists expect him to return at any time. But where has he been in the meantime? Colossians 3:1 tells us: "Seek those things which are above, where Christ is, sitting at the right hand of God." This places the Father and the Son somewhere above us, with Jesus located on the right side of his dad. Where then do we find the Holy Spirit? Corinthians 6:19 says " your body is the temple of the Holy Spirit, who is in you." So the Bible tells us that God the Holy Spirit is exactly where you are at this moment-sitting inside of you!

We have seen God the Father's anger issues. In contrast, the Holy Spirit is quiet and humble. He has no story to promote and no image to uphold. His qualities include a loving nature (Romans 15:30), deep knowledge (I Corinthians 2:10-11), and helpfulness (Romans 8:26). God as the Son shows us the futility of worshipping God as another human being. This has caused incredible suffering- countless millions of people have died during wars waged in Jesus' name. Seek God where the Bible tells us that God is- in you! It's all about the Holy Spirit. Blasphemy against the Holy Spirit is the failure to recognize that God is in you, which will unforgivingly blind you to the truth of your true nature as pure divine awareness.

III. It's All God and It's Always Now

In Exodus 3:14 God simply tells us "I am that I am." Deuteronomy 6:4 further elaborates: "Hear O Israel-the Lord our God, the Lord is one." So God is that which is, and that which is is one. Switching from the Old to the New Testament, Jesus adds that "the Father and I are one." Jesus was aware that he and his father are one, and so is everything else. After all, Jesus' father is that which is!

Jesus tells us in Matthew 6:25-34 "do not worry about your life, what you will eat or what you will drink; nor about your body, what you will put on... do not worry saying 'What shall we eat?' or 'What shall we drink?' or 'What shall we wear?'...Seek first the Kingdom of God and all these things shall be added to you. Therefore, do not worry about tomorrow, for tomorrow will worry about its own things."

If Jesus meant what he said, his core message was "embrace the present moment, ignore the folly of focusing on the past or projecting into the future." The Bible then becomes a treasure hunt for jewels of harmonious wisdom like Psalms 46:10 which tells us "Be still, and know that I am God." The insanity of future speculation is demonstrated for us in the disturbing imagery of the Book of Revelation.

The Three Key Verses Revisited

I recently returned to the three key Bible verses I had been given to memorize as a fundamentalist. They also can be understood from an enlightened perspective. This is not surprising, as Jesus of Nazareth was an enlightened spiritual teacher.

1. JOHN 3:3: When Jesus said that one needs to be born again to see the Kingdom of God, just what exactly did he mean? I recently asked two Overstory-indoctrinated acquaintances to define the term "born again." One responded "it means that you have a personal relationship with Jesus Christ." Another answered "it means that I am no longer number one in my life- Jesus is." After hearing these answers, I had no more useful information than before I had asked in the first place.

The true meaning of John 3:3 must be viewed through the context of Jesus' humility, compassion and charity- his connectedness. What he spoke of was rebirth from the misery of the illusion of separation into a state of conscious unity with everyone and everything. That is to be born again- the transition from being apart from everything to the experience of being a part of everything.

[58]

2. JOHN 3:16: The love which would have been necessary for God to send his son to help humanity is not always present in the Bible. In Genesis 6:7 the same God says "I will destroy...both man and beast...for I am sorry I have made them." At that point in time God so loathed the world that he flooded it- sparing only Noah, his family and the collection they took on the ark.

Who changed between the time of Noah and the time of Jesus- humanity or its angry God? The answer is God, and what John 3:16 tells us is that "God GREW to so love the world that he sent his only begotten Son." Otherwise, the Bible leaves us with a God whose love is on-again, off-again and catastrophically unpredictable.

3. JOHN 14:6: This is where Jesus says "I am the way...no one comes to the Father except through Me." Ironically, this verse is frequently used to promote the spiritual bigotry of the religious right. By taking this statement in the most-narrow minded manner conceivable, fundamentalists teach that the "Me" Jesus referred to was the extremely limited illustration of God as that individual human being. But why would God ever refer to himself in a self-limiting way?

To God in the fullest sense, the Father is a limited illustration of the limitless being he (it) actually is. The person of God the Son is even narrower. The "Me" speaking through Jesus is the limitless Holy Spirit. What is said in John 14:6 is "God without limits is the way, and the truth, and the light. No one can understand the limited illustration of God as Father until he or she can recognize the limitless nature of the Holy Spirit."

No collection of writings, no matter how handsomely bound, is worthy of the blind idolatry I was told to attach to the Bible. Even among those calling themselves Christians, there is nothing close to unanimous interpretation of the books it contains. The modern fundamentalist must attach an elaborate and peculiar explanation to the Bible- an Overstory which disrespects science and the philosophies and traditions of others.

At this point, we will examine these four essential questions:

1. Which writings are included in the Bible and what is their significance?

2. Are all Christian Bibles the same?

3. Which related writings were not included it the Bible and what did they say?

4. Who decided what the Bible would contain and when was it decided?

THE WRITINGS INCLUDED IN THE BIBLE

The Bible was written by an unknown number of people, and is said to cover a period from the beginning of time to an uncertain date in the near future. The people who recorded its 66 books thought they were living on a flat earth at the center of the universe. From this background emerges the Bible- a collection of ancient folklore, poems, history and speculation.

The Books of the Old Testament

The Pentateuch (or Torah)

Modern historians estimate that Moses died around 1250 BCE, although fundamentalist theologians place his death hundreds of years earlier. The writing of first five books of the Old Testament (also known as the Torah) began around 950 BCE, shortly after the death of King David. While fundamentalists claim that Moses wrote these books, they were probably not completed until about 600 BCE.

1. GENESIS: This book supposedly begins about 6000 years ago when the Overstory tells us that the universe was created. Historically this book traces the roots of Judaism, Christianity and Islam through the story of Abraham, who may have actually existed circa

1850 BCE.

2. EXODUS: The Jews are lead by Moses from slavery in Egypt toward a destiny of greatness.

3. LEVITICUS: The demands and requirements of an angry and violent God are spelled out.

4. NUMBERS: Forty years of desert wandering between Egyptian slavery and the promised land. A great deal of human slaughter is necessary to satisfy God.

5. DEUTERONOMY: This account of Moses' career and forty years of desert wandering was probably written by the prophet Jeremiah around 620 BCE. Deuteronomy is suspiciously harmonious with Jeremiah's prophetic writings, and he was active when this book was "discovered."

The Historical Books

The twelve books which follow are not objective historical accounts. Rather, they were attempts by their authors to weave Jewish folklore into the perspective of the times in which they were written.

6. JOSHUA: A moral and scientific mess. Joshua 10:12-14 provides a good example. Here God orders the sun to stand still for 24 hours to give the Israelites around the clock daylight to mercilessly slaughter the Amorites. The author was ignorant of the later-discovered fact that night and day result from the earth spinning on its axis. If that were ever halted, the gravitational effect would instantly destroy the earth.

7. JUDGES: Another writing from Jeremiah and/or his contemporaries. An essay on the majesty of Yahweh, the high standards of Jewish worship and the need to resist foreign influence.

8. RUTH: Now viewed as satire by many scholars, the Book of Ruth reveals that King David's great-grandmother was a heathen.

[61]

Such a person could not have lived in Jerusalem when this book was written. Ten generations of pure Jewish blood were then required, a quorum which David did not meet.

9. I SAMUEL: The Jewish royal era begins. I Samuel covers a little over 100 years through its three main characters- Samuel, Saul and David.

10. II SAMUEL: King David takes Israel to the pinnacle of its glory. I and II Samuel were probably written three or four hundred years after the events they describe.

11. I KINGS: David dies and passes the throne of a great and united Jewish kingdom to his son, Solomon. A wise but prideful man, Solomon builds a great temple in Jerusalem and a vast palace for himself. Decline gradually sets in, and the kingdom is divided during the reign of his son, Rehoboam.

12. II KINGS: The decline continues. The northern Hebrew kingdom of Israel falls to the Assyrians in 722 BCE and by 586 BCE the southern kingdom of Judah is enslaved by King Nebuchadnezzar of Babylon.

13. I CHRONICLES: Chronicles is a parallel history to Kings, but written from the humbler perspective of Jewish Babylonian captivity. I Chronicles begins with Adam and ends with David.

14. II CHRONICLES: Starts with the reign of Solomon and ends with the fall of Jerusalem to Nebuchadnezzar. I and II Chronicles attempt to answer why God's chosen people had earned his wrath.

15. EZRA: King Cyrus of Babylon allows the captive Jewish people to return to Jerusalem. Some do, including Ezra the great leader, historian and scribe. This book is a favorite of fundamentalists because it stresses "God's one true religion."

16. NEHEMIAH: Like Ezra, Nehemiah was a priest in Jerusalem immediately after the Babylonian captivity. This book recounts the rebuilding of the walls of the Jewish holy city and calls for Jewish national purity and strict adherence to Hebrew law.

17. ESTHER: The story of a Jewish woman who marries the King of Persia and thwarts a royal minister's plot to destroy the Jews. This book is not corroborated by secular history.

The Poetical and Wisdom Books

These writings, along with the Book of Esther, were probably the last books of the Old Testament to be written. With the possible exception of Job all were produced after the Babylonian exile ended in 539 BCE.

18. JOB: Based on the outline of an ancient story about the tribulations of a righteous man, the Book of Job did not reach its present form until perhaps 550 BCE. Modern scholars view the story as a protest against the teachings in Proverbs that hard work and high morals will earn God's favor.

19. PSALMS: A collection of poems from a variety of sources. Some of them can be traced to Egypt, Samaria and Canaan. A handful are probably from the time of David, circa 975 BCE, to whom fundamentalists credit the majority of the writing. Most of them are now dated between 539 and 500 BCE.

20. PROVERBS: A collection of wise sayings traditionally attributed to Solomon, but probably written centuries after his death. Put simply, life according to Proverbs means that wise living will bring prosperity and happiness.

21. ECCLESIASTES: Perhaps not completed in its present form until as late as 300 BCE, this book provides a Greek-influenced probe into the meaning of life. Ecclesiastes' almost godless tone has caused Jewish scholars to question its place as scripture.

22. SONG OF SOLOMON: A series of erotic love poems which had little to do with God or Jewish religion when they were composed.

The writers who became known as the Old Testament prophets were not attempting to predict the future when they composed their writings. That explanation was assigned much later, when early Christians were adding details to the story of Jesus. During their own time the so-called prophets merely sought to place everyone and everything under the dominion of their God.

23. ISAIAH: Isaiah promises the arrival of a royal Jewish child called Immanuel. This book addressed a difficult time in Judea some 700 years before Jesus was born.

24. JEREMIAH: Jeremiah is known as the prophet who predicted Jesus' birth to a virgin. An accurate translation of the Hebrew word "almah," which he used in his writing, has been shown by modern linguists to mean "young woman" rather than "virgin."

25. LAMENTATIONS: Also written by Jeremiah, the book is most accurately described as a sampling of disturbing poems. In them, God shows himself to be pathologically angry and judgmental.

26. EZEKIEL: Emphasizing the restoration of Israel, passages from this book are used by modern Christians obsessed with so-called end times prophecy. Like Isaiah and Jeremiah, Ezekiel tells of an angry and violent God.

27. DANIEL: Set during the Babylonian captivity of the sixth century BCE, the Book of Daniel was probably written after 200 BCE. It influenced the writing of the Book of Revelation some 300 years later. Chapters 7 and 12 of Daniel are favorites among Christians prone to predicting the exact date of the end of the world.

28. HOSEA: God tells Hosea to marry a harlot and the righteous prophet obeys. Despite her chronic infidelity, the man never stops loving his wayward bride. This writing is said to illustrate God's love for his people despite their chronic sinning.

29. JOEL: A graphic description of a great plague of locusts in

Judah. Joel underscores the fundamentalist teaching that God punishes nations which fall out of his favor.

30. AMOS: This prophet preached a message of charity and social justice. Amos' enlightened priorities are underemphasized, if not overlooked entirely, by much of the present-day religious right.

31. OBADIAH: Emphasizing the doom of the proud and the deliverance of the humble, Obadiah is the shortest book of the Old Testament.

32. JONAH: A tale of repentance. Jonah disobeys God and is cast into the sea, spending three days inside the belly of a large fish. He emerges at Nineveh to proclaim God's mercy to the heathens there.

33. MICAH: This prophet was an enlightened country lawyer who strove for social justice during his own time. His hope that Bethlehem, birthplace of David, might one day produce another great Jewish king influenced later accounts of the life of Jesus of Nazareth.

34. NAHUM: This brief book again shows God to be jealous, angry, and indignant. Written about 150 years after Jonah was said to have delivered Nineveh to righteousness, Nahum describes its destruction as divine retribution for Nineveh's return to its evil ways.

35. HABAKKUK: A look at God's ways written during the time that Babylon dominated the Middle East. Wondering aloud why bad men prosper and tragic events are allowed to take place, Habakkuk calls out to his creator "how long shall I cry and you not hear?"

36. ZEPHANIAH: A message against idolatry which darkly promises the coming of the dreadful "day of the Lord." God promises in Zephaniah 1:2-3 to "utterly consume everything" and "cut off man from the face of the land."

37. HAGGAI: A call to rebuild the temple in Jerusalem following seventy years of captivity in Babylon. Haggai viewed the period of captivity as God's punishment for Judah's failure to observe religious law.

38. ZECHARIAH: A contemporary of Haggai's. Zechariah's imagery influenced New Testament accounts of Jesus of Nazareth and John the Baptist.

39. MALACHI: Another post-Babylonian writing which angrily criticizes immorality and indifference to God, even among the Jews.

The Books of the New Testament

The Gospels

Perhaps as many as 200 gospels were written in the two centuries after Jesus was crucified. Four of these accounts, produced between 75 and 120 CE, were declared Bible canon some 350 years after the events they portray. A forgiving and nonviolent Son of God dominates Matthew, Mark, Luke and John. Some details about his life and death were borrowed from the Old Testament prophets.

1. MATTHEW: Probably written circa 80 CE, this book explains Jewish history and tradition through the person of Jesus. Relying on Mark as his primary source, Matthew promotes Jesus as the Jewish Messiah and includes a substantial majority of all New Testament references to hell.

2. MARK: The oldest of the four included gospels, written around 75 CE, Mark shows a world of demonic forces being challenged by Jesus. The earliest manuscripts of the Book of Mark end at Chapter 16, verse 8, before the resurrected Jesus appears to his disciples and ascends into heaven. These details were added much later in order to conform with the other three gospels.

3. LUKE: Like Matthew, Luke was written in the early 80s CE with Mark as a strong influence. It's author, a Greek, goes to great lengths to avoid offending the Roman leadership which had destroyed Jerusalem in the year 70. In Luke, Roman procurator Pontius Pilate proclaims Jesus innocent and only very reluctantly allows the crucifixion to take place. Despite the political pander-

ing, this gospel is well-written and offers several stories not found elsewhere.

4. JOHN: Recorded circa 120 CE, John's miracle-rich gospel was a response to rising doubts about Christianity in the face of Jesus' ongoing failure to return to earth. Faith in Jesus as the Jewish Messiah had waned greatly in the 50 years since the Roman destruction of Jerusalem. John took the first major step toward the later creation of the Trinity by calling Jesus "the Word" and adding that "the Word was God."

5. THE ACTS OF THE APOSTLES: Acts is not a gospel but a unique book written by Luke around 90 CE. Paul's Greek traveling companion shares a colorful recount of the years between the crucifixion, circa 28 CE, and Paul's execution in the year 65. There are discrepancies between Luke's details and those earlier offered by Paul in his letters.

The Letters of Paul

While Paul was the largest contributor to the New Testament, several writings traditionally credited to him are now known to have been composed at least a generation after his death. His genuine letters offered simple advice to various churches as they awaited the return of Jesus at any moment. Paul's epistles were the first New Testament books written when they were composed between 50 and 64 CE. He did not intend to write anything which would ever be considered scripture and indicated no knowledge of later-added gospel detail concerning Jesus' life and career.

6. ROMANS: Paul tells how God makes sinners good in his own eyes, and also insists that "every soul be subject to the governing authorities (Roman 13:1)." This passage has been frequently abused by Christian tyrants over the centuries.

7. I CORINTHIANS: Paul's favorite church experiences compromise with the carnal world. About 54 CE Paul forwarded this letter which includes several comments on the ungodly nature of

human sexuality.

8. II CORINTHIANS: Paul shares more of his personal experience in this writing than in any other. Composed around 57 CE, it was probably the third in a series of letters which started with I Corinthians. This epistle refers to a previous "painful letter" which cannot logically be considered a reference to I Corinthians.

9. GALATIANS: Probably the earliest of the New Testament books, dated at roughly 50 CE. Paul's movement away from Judaism is strongly evident. Twenty-odd years after Jesus' death divisions between the new religion and its Jewish foundation are already showing.

10. EPHISIANS: Likely written by Paul's followers about 90 CE. A companion piece to some of Paul's earlier authentic letters.

11. PHILLIPIANS: A letter Paul composed to thank a group of Christians for their financial support while he was imprisoned. Perhaps a composite of more than one correspondence.

12. COLOSSIANS: Perhaps truly Paul's writing, perhaps not. A treatise on baptismal symbols and false teachings.

13. I THESSALONIANS: Written by Paul at the dawn of the 50s CE, I Thessalonians shares details of the day when Jesus will come back. His narrative includes the rising of dead believers passionately anticipated by fundamentalists in the present day.

14. II THESSALONIANS: More about the second coming and Jesus' enemies. Some modern experts suspect this letter was written by students of Paul circa 95 CE.

15. I TIMOTHY: This letter was probably produced at least 60 years after Paul died. Instructions for church leadership and warnings about false teachings were put in Paul's mouth to give these words greater influence.

16. II TIMOTHY: Like I Timothy, this letter appears to be advice to a young pastor. It was written by the same people who wrote the first letter.

17. TITUS: Historically similar to the two contrived Timothy letters. This "letter from Paul to Titus" refers to a church structure which was not yet in place when Paul was alive.

18. PHILEMON: Authentically Paul's, written around 55 CE. Odd because it is written to an individual rather than a church and deals with a practical situation (a runaway slave) rather than theological issues.

The General Epistles and Revelation

When the contents of the New Testament were finally settled on they included a small group of writings which were not gospels and not credited to Paul. They were:

19. HEBREWS: The earliest known manuscripts of this book attribute it to Paul. By the early third century Church fathers admitted that its author was not known. Dated at around 125 CE, the text of Hebrews shows influence from the Gospel of John and Psalm 110 as it portrays Jesus as a man from heaven who had existed prior to his birth.

20. JAMES: While written around 100 CE, James' collection of moral instructions did not gain wide Church acceptance until after the year 300. Attributed to Jesus' brother, its actual authorship is not certain.

21. I PETER: This epistle to Christians experiencing persecution in Turkey was composed around 90 CE. Credited to Peter some 25 years after he had died, the letter was likely written by someone wanting to combine Paul's writing style with the authority of Peter.

22. II PETER: Written at least 25 years after I Peter, this book is a treatise against false teachings from the perspective of an orthodoxy which did not exist during Peter's own time.

23. I JOHN: Written about the same time as the Gospel of John (about 120 CE) and likely by the same person or people who composed it. This writing addresses a gentile Christian community

which had fully separated itself from Judaism.

24. II JOHN: Probably from a different author than I John, this book discusses Christian love.

25. III JOHN: Almost certainly from the same source as II John, III John shows the growing organizational sophistication of the Christian church circa 130 CE.

26. JUDE: This brief letter from around the year 100 has been attributed to Jesus' brother Judas (not Iscariot), who was also known as Jude. Its rallying cry against "false teachers" shows that, at the turn of the second century, the essence of so-called Christian truth was still very much up for grabs.

27. REVELATION: Not generally considered canon until the fourth century. Some in the early Church considered this odd book the legitimate work of John Zebedee. Perhaps just as many dismissed it as the ranting of the heretic Cerenthus.

DIFFERENCES IN PRESENT-DAY CHRISTIAN BIBLES

As are now aware, reasonable minds can differ on the authorship and significance of the books of the Bible. Reasonable (as well as unreasonable) Christian churches also disagree over what it contains in the first place. The Bible used by all Protestants includes the 66 books discussed above. The Bibles of the Roman Catholic and Greek Orthodox Christian Churches differ as follows:

The Roman Catholic Bible: Includes all of the 66 above-listed books and seven Old Testament offerings not present in the Protestant version-Tobit, Judith, I and II Maccabees, Wisdom, Sirach and Baruch.

The Greek Orthodox Bible: In addition to all of the books present in the Roman Catholic version, the Greek Orthodox Old Testament also includes I Esdras, III and IV Maccabees, Odes, Psalms of Solomon and the Letter of Jeremiah.

The Roman Catholic and Greek Orthodox Bibles also include 103 more verses in the Book of Esther and three more sections in the Book of Daniel than the Protestant version. The Greek Orthodox Bible also includes one more Psalm than do the Catholic or Protestant Bibles. While the New Testament used by all three traditions is the same, this was very nearly not the case. Protestant patriarch Martin Luther wished to remove the books of Hebrews, James, Jude and Revelation. Despite his vast influence, this ultimately did not happen.

RELATED WRITINGS NOT INCLUDED IN THE BIBLE

Scores, if not hundreds, of Jewish and Christian holy books were written between the close of the Old Testament period and the official listing of the Christian Bible in the year 367. Of the wealth of related writings which did not make the final New Testament cut, I have included summaries of ten personal favorites. They are:

1. THE INFANCY GOSPEL OF THOMAS: Written at about the same time as the Gospel of John, this account of Jesus' early years enjoyed widespread popularity. In it, the boy Jesus makes clay sparrows come to life, withers playmates he doesn't like and calls his dad Joseph "stupid" for reprimanding him.

2. THE GOSPEL OF JUDAS: This gospel reveals a secret conversation between Jesus and the man said to be his betrayer. Jesus thanks Judas Iscariot for freeing him from his body and assures Judas that facilitating the crucifixion was a noble and heroic act.

3. THE GOSPEL OF NICODEMUS: Purported to be the official account of the arrest, trial and crucifixion of Jesus of Nazareth. This book also details Jesus' appearance in hell and the subsequent arrest of Satan.

4. THE GOSPEL OF THOMAS: Written circa 90 CE, this gospel was especially popular in Syria. It is a collection of sayings, proverbs, parables and prophecies from the mouth of Jesus.

5. THE GOSPEL OF THE HEBREWS: A gospel which was writ-

ten in Greek and favored by Christians of a Jewish background.

6. THE GOSPEL OF BARTHOLOMEW: Jesus frees Adam, Eve and other worthy souls from captivity in hell. Jesus tells Bartholomew that for every 30,000 souls which leave the earth, only three will reach heaven.

7. THE ACTS OF PETER: A Christ-empowered Peter competes with the devil in a miracle working contest held at the Roman Forum. The devil loses, and is stoned by the crowd. Peter's run of luck is short lived- after falling into the disfavor of local authorities, he is crucified upside down.

8. THE ACTS OF JOHN: In this book John heals the sick, raises the dead and successfully orders bedbugs to stop disturbing his sleep. He also forgives sins and destroys a pagan temple at Ephesus.

9. THE APOCALYPSE OF PAUL: Paul visits the heavenly city of Christ and finds it protected by 12 walls and 12,000 towers. Inside it is full of fruit trees and God is briefed every day by angels about noteworthy human activity. Based on these reports God decides who will later live in the heavenly city and who will spend eternity in hell.

10. THE APOCALYPSE OF PETER: Peter is allowed to view God's coming day of judgment in which the gates of hell are opened and the earth and stars are destroyed by fire. Heaven is shown as a place with never-fading flowers, while hell is full of tortured fornicators.

THE SELECTION OF THE BOOKS OF THE BIBLE

The Judaism from which Christianity sprang has a strong written tradition. Nevertheless, the writings of the Old Testament were not settled upon until 90 CE during a council of rabbis at Jamnia. Even supposing that all of the Old Testament was intended by its authors to survive for thousands of years, no such argument can be made for the contents of the New Testament.

When Jesus was executed in about 28 CE no one was more surprised than his followers. They scattered after their Messiah had unexpectedly failed to overthrow Roman rule. After Peter became convinced that Jesus had risen from the dead, he and his group did not anticipate a long absence. Stories about Jesus were spread by word of mouth and no significant Christian writing took place until about 50 CE.

The Christian storytelling tradition was gradually augmented with letters passed between the various churches. Some of them (the writings of Paul for example) carried greater weight than others. By the year 100 a wide variety of accounts of Jesus' life and ministry were also being circulated. Now known as gospels, they became more important as the second century progressed and Jesus was still inexplicably absent.

By about the year 140, over a century after the time of Jesus, a prominent Roman Christian known as Marcion set out to establish an official list of recognized Christian writings. Marcion excluded the Old Testament altogether, and included only the Gospel of Luke and 10 letters from Paul in his proposed holy Christian canon. After excommunicating Marcion in 144 for his negative ideas about the God of the Jews (he suggested that the father of Jesus had been a different god altogether), Roman Church leaders began to more seriously consider which writings should be embraced by their organization. By about the year 180 Irenaeus, the influential Bishop of Lyons, suggested that since are four winds and four points on a compass that four official gospels would be an appropriate number. By the dawn of the third century Matthew, Mark, Luke and John were emerging as the favored four in many circles.

As time went by the various churches requested an official roster of writings for use in worship services and as a guide for living. The first list naming the 27 books of today's New Testament was produced in 367 CE by Athanasius the Bishop of Alexandria. In 393 the Synod of Hippo officially approved Athanasius' list, and that is how the Christian Bible as we know it came to be.

The popular impression that the New Testament is a collection of unique writings produced by eyewitnesses to the life of Jesus is simply not true. Its 27 books are typical of a vast number of writings produced over a long period of time, each of them reflecting the limitations of the times and places in which they were created.

The mythical image of Moses receiving the Ten Commandments directly from Yahweh on stone tablets (Exodus 24:12) is a powerful one. Modern fundamentalists extend the same "direct from the hand of God" outlook to all of the writings which are now bound up in the Bible. Their book idolatry experience is enhanced by special Bible bindings, paper textures and the arbitrary division of the books into chapters and verses. Such divisions were not finalized until 1551.

The leaders of my former church attach the far-fetched Overstory to a tragically misunderstood collection of writings. Still, in a certain way, the Bible is true. It is true to what it actually is. It just isn't what the fundamentalists tell us it is.

CHAPTER 5
DEALING WITH THE DEVIL

Beyond Myth, Superstition and Fear

Just a few miles from where I live stands the Institute for Creation Research's Museum of Creation and Earth History. This fascinating collection of exhibits in Santee, California came highly recommended during my 1990s fundamentalist period, but somehow I never had occasion to visit until the afternoon of January 23, 2008.

The museum was bigger and better organized than I had imagined before my visit, and several predictable points were driven home with elaborate displays. These displays, in turn, were amplified with quotes from Genesis and other scripture. Promoting the literal accuracy of the Bible and exposing flaws in the theory of evolution and scientific carbon fossil dating give the museum its purpose .

One display in particular caught my attention. The Great Flood exhibit trumpeted the "literal truth" of chapters 6 through 9 of the Book of Genesis. It explained how fragments of the story spread to Middle Eastern pagan cultures and beyond. This was attributed to Genesis Chapter 11 which tells us that there was only one human language before the Tower of Babel episode. At that point God scattered humanity over the face of the earth and different groups began speaking different languages. According to my hosts, bits and pieces of "God's truth" were shared in new pagan languages, including some details of Noah's Great Flood.

The obvious conclusion that great flood stories were part of a common ancient mythology would overrule the Overstory. Fundamentalists therefore insist that the ancient folklore included in the Bible is objective fact. Over the past several centuries the modern scientific method has revealed the falsehood of classic mythology. In response today's fundamentalists promote Bible myths as science and legitimate science as secular myth.

The creation story and related Bible mythology has become a problem which Protestant Christianity did not foresee when it set out to de-mystify Catholicism during the sixteen century. With the arrival of the printing press (circa 1450) and growing literacy, the Protestant Reformation of Luther and Calvin encouraged the reading of the Bible. After 1000 years of hearing only bits of scripture recited in Latin during Catholic mass, Western Christians began to use the entire Bible as literally reliable information.

A new faith in reason created a conflict between faith and science which still rages today. Modern science, however, did not set out to discredit faith. In fact, astronomer Nicolas Copernicus (1473-1543) saw his work as a religious activity and was disturbed to discover that the earth was not at the center of the universe as his Church had always insisted. Later British advocates of reason like Francis Bacon (1561-1626) and Isaac Newton (1642-1727), while believers, sought to separate science and mythology. Enlightened Christians came to recognize that the Bible includes ancient mythology, while the less progressive still insist that science is off base. To this day, Christian fundamentalists reject the obvious conclusion that the myths recorded in the Bible are actually myths. Some of them even build museums.

After my visit to the Museum of Creation and Earth History, I became curious about the following questions:

1. How was the Old Testament influenced by mythology?

2. Is mythology also present in the New Testament?

3. How is superstition distinguished from spirituality?

4. What are the origins of hell, Satan, demons and eternal punishment?

[76]

MYTHOLOGY AND THE OLD TESTAMENT

From a regional background of creation myths and great floods came the Israelites. Though influenced by the religious traditions of Canaan, Egypt and Babylon, they were closer to nearby tribes such as the Ammonites, Edomites and Moabites. These groups all had dominant male gods. A great deal of history-flavored Hebrew mythology came into being as justification for their disturbingly violent conquest of the Canaanites. As told by the Old Testament historical books the God of Abraham preferred the Jews over all other people on earth. Terrible violence against the people of Canaan was justified by God's mythological covenant with Abraham which continued through Isaac, Jacob and Moses.

At the center of early Semitic mythology was El, a very ancient creator/father god from whom Yahweh inherited many characteristics. El's wife was Ashura the earth goddess. Before the first five chapters of the Old Testament finally took shape around 600 BCE the Jews worshipped not only Ashura but also Syria's patriarch Baal and Babylon's love goddess Ishtar alongside Yahweh.

During the time of Jeremiah (circa 600 BCE) a new generation of Jewish leaders rejected all gods other than Yahweh, and trivialized them in writings like Psalm 82 where Yahweh "judges among the gods." This period provided mythological status to actual Jewish historical figures like Joshua, David and Josiah. A new Jewish loathing of once respected (and sometimes worshipped) pagan gods is clear in writings such as II Chronicles, chapter 34. Here, King Josiah purges Judah of all Baal-oriented worship paraphernalia on behalf of a new Yahweh-only Judaism.

In roughly six centuries between the time of Jeremiah and the ministry of Jesus of Nazareth a series of foreign powers dominated the Jewish people. A growing mythology surrounding David in particular led to anticipation of a Jewish Messiah who would lead the Jews to freedom from Persian (538-333 BCE), Greek (332-142 BCE) and finally Roman rule which began in 63 BCE. During the Roman period growing groups of Jews actively promoted the arrival of a Messiah who would eliminate foreign influence from the holy land and usher in a Kingdom of God which would be ruled directly by Yahweh. It was from this movement that Jesus emerged.

CHRISTIANITY, MYTHOLOGY
AND THE NEW TESTAMENT

Jesus was one of many would-be Messiahs in Roman Palestine during his time. He came from a line of Kingdom of God activists which included Judah the Galilean and his personal mentor, John the Baptist. Jesus' public humiliation and death by crucifixion at the hands of Imperial Rome was completely out of line with Jewish messianic expectations. Nevertheless, after Jesus was executed Peter and his followers began telling of a risen Jesus who had gone back to his father, but would very soon return to introduce the Kingdom of God.

By the time Paul began his known writings (circa 50 CE), Christian mythology was evolving. Showing no particular interest in the details of Jesus' life or the content of his teachings, Paul instead connected a man of history with an ancient mythological tradition of heroes who had died and risen to new life. A generation and more after Paul, the New Testament gospels harmonized the supposed details of Jesus' life with Old Testament messianic mythology. As we saw in chapter two, much of the biblical detail about the life of Jesus of Nazareth was almost certainly contrived to tie the Christian movement to the history of Judaism.

Gentile mythology was added to the new faith as Christianity became a largely non-Jewish movement. Obvious pagan influence found its way into the religion, a fact that did not go unnoticed by early Christian leaders. In the late second century the pagan humorist and philosopher Celcus expressed the opinion that Christianity was an inferior recycling of familiar mythology. The early Church even admitted the similarities- then blamed the devil for copying Jesus' life story in advance!

The parallels between the Jesus of the Bible and earlier mythological figures is striking. One figure in particular influenced the New

Testament to a vast extent- Osiris, an ancient Egyptian godman who died and rose from the dead. The same basic figure was known as Dionysus in Greece, Adonis in Syria, Attis in Asia Minor, Bacchus on the Italian peninsula and Mithras in Persia. The subject of Gnostic and mythological influences on early Christianity has been documented by authors Timothy Freke and Peter Gandy in their book "The Jesus Mysteries." Among others, they point out these similarities:

(1) Jesus Had a Human Virgin Mother: So did Adonis, Attis and Dionysus.

(2) Jesus' Father was a Celestial God: So were the fathers of Bacchus and Dionysus, the Son of Zeus.

(3) Jesus was Born on December 25 with Three Shepherds Present: So was Mithras. While Christianity adopted the birth date after the New Testament was written, the presence of the shepherds is reported in the Gospel of Luke.

(4) Jesus Performed Miracles: So did Dionysus, including turning water into wine. Asclepius, the Greek god of medicine and son of Apollo, healed those who were sick and brought the dead back to life.

(5) Jesus Traveled with Twelve Disciples: So did Osiris and Dionysus.

(6) Jesus Rode on a Donkey on the Way to Meet His Fate: The same was again true of Dionysus.

(7) Jesus was Betrayed for Thirty Pieces of Silver: The same detail is present in the story of the Greek philosopher Socrates, who actually existed some 450 years before Jesus.

(8) Jesus Initiated a Bread and Wine Ritual Prior to His Death: So did Mithras.

(9) Jesus was Executed to Atone for the Sins of Humanity: As was Dionysus, who like Jesus pointed out that his persecutors knew not what they were doing.

(10) Jesus' Followers await His Return: So did the followers of Osiris and Dionysus.

Clearly, the new Christian movement sold itself to the Gentile world with familiar symbols and stories. This allowed non-Jewish converts to recognize Jesus as a godman on terms they could understand.

SUPERSTITION VERSUS SPIRITUALITY

Merriam-Webster defines "superstition" as follows:

1a. A belief or practice resulting from ignorance, fear of the unknown, trust in magic or chance, or a false conception of causation. 1b. An irrational abject attitude of mind toward the supernatural, nature or God resulting from superstition. 2. A notion maintained despite evidence to the contrary (merriam-webster.com).

A few years ago a friend told me about her grandmother, a superstitious woman from a simple background in rural Mexico. She laughed while sharing that her grandmother shut all of her kitchen cupboards tightly before retiring each night. This was done because the old woman feared that evil spirits would come out of open cupboards late at night and cause unwanted mischief. Going back to Merriam-Webster's definition of superstition this would seem to fit perfectly as a "belief...resulting from ignorance (or) fear of the unknown."

I heard another straight-faced testimonial to a false conception of causation a few months back. An otherwise reasonable middle aged man shared that God had caused divorce papers filed by his wife to disappear before they could be served upon him. The possibility that the lovesick husband had helped God lose these documents aside, he appears to be an otherwise sane individual. As a believer in the Overstory, however, he embraces a deity who tricks process servers every bit as effectively as evil spirits from a cupboard ever could.

As for "notion(s) maintained despite evidence to the contrary (definition #2, above)," we need look no further than my recent visit to the Museum of Creation and Earth History. It's promoters insist that if there is a God at all the Book of Genesis must be literally accurate. All compelling science to the contrary, these fundamentalists cannot bring themselves to admit that the Bible's creation story is a mythical seven-day illustration of a process which actually took billions of years.

There has to be a logical reason for the stubborn, persistent appeal of superstition in the information age, and there is:

Superstition: Me, We, Superman and Santa Claus

Chuck Chamberlain pointed out that the human ego is "the one problem that includes all problems." He went on to define ego as "the feeling of conscious separation from everything (else)." The core problem with Christian fundamentalism is that it panders to the ego. Ironically, this strengthens the estrangement from God it claims to eliminate in the first place. By encouraging every separate little "me" to establish a separate "personal relationship with God" a person's perspective on the universe is so selfishly skewed that superstitious beliefs and practices seem logical.

Think about it. There are well over six and one half billion human beings on earth as of this writing. A disturbingly high percentage of them don't have enough food to make it through the day. As some of them starve, Christian fundamentalists in our society often pray for the trappings of material affluence. This is done in reliance upon a supernatural relationship with a godman who said "sell whatever you have and give it to the poor (Mark 10:21)." Obviously it is not a personal relationship with Jesus' specific teachings they are seeking. On the contrary, preferred status with a Superman/Santa Claus figure is the object of the game. Their idol's Superman qualities can drive away trouble while his Santa Claus side will respond to the endless demands of the separate little me. At the end of the game the ego is whisked away to eternal paradise.

Sometimes even the ego and its god are not enough to quench the desires, and especially fears, of the separate me. Often a "we" of varying natures, sizes and durations becomes necessary. For example, if a space invasion threatened our planet all religious and political rivalries would be set aside until the threat had passed. Then matters like religion and politics would reclaim the ego's attention. The availability of whatever sized "we" the ego happens to need continues down through identification with city, street, and family- but the me is usually more important than any imaginable we. The individual ego typically trumps all other bonds, including those of blood.

Consider the fear the ego must entertain in order to affix itself to the Overstory. Accepting the fundamentalist reality has its rewards- the little ego-me is told that it will live forever in heaven. But at what cost? Suspension of reason in exchange for the avoidance of mythological torture in a fiery fictitious hell.

Spirituality: Recognizing and Embracing Animating Energy

Returning to Merriam-Webster, we examine the first definition of the word spirit: "an animating or vital principle held to give life to physical organisms." This vital principle animates all things and has nothing to do with the fears and demands of any individual. On this point, Chuck Chamberlain elaborated "If (something is) important to me personally, its an ego satisfaction. If I am praying right it is not for something for me. It is that I might be of some value to you."

Superstition can be readily separated from spirituality. Spirituality embraces and deepens the connection to everyone and everything else. Superstition finds a little me requesting favors for itself or for the groups with which it identifies. Be it closing cupboards tightly at night to contain evil spirits or asking the Christian God for more money, superstition is superstition.

THE DEVIL AND HIS REALM:
A MYTHOLOGICAL EVOLUTION

One of many derisive terms I learned as a fundamentalist was the label "fire insurance Christian." Roughly speaking, the zealots view Christians of this variety as not being on fire for Jesus but as doing just enough to avoid the fire of hell. They are seen as being motivated by fear to do the minimum necessary rather than motivated by a passion to spread the gospel.

Even in the twenty-first century it is difficult to fully gage the role that fear plays in the promotion of fundamentalist Christianity. It is certainly a considerable factor, as it has been from the beginning. The details of a Jesus versus Satan, heaven versus hell duality has its roots in mythology much older than even the Judaism from which Christianity emerged. This dark side of Christianity evolved as follows:

Pre-Christian Demonology

Over 4000 years ago the gods of what is now Iraq were said to send evil people to a fiery place full of demons. Such a fate was also feared by ancient Egyptians as the destination of souls lacking in good works. In Zoroastrianism, which became popular in the Middle East about 500 BCE, evildoers found themselves after death in a hell ruled by an evil spirit known as Ahriman. This hell, however, would one day be destroyed by a savior known as Saoshyant. Perhaps not surprisingly, the mother of Saoshyant was believed to be a virgin.

The Greeks also left a clear mark on the dark side of Christian mythology. According to Greek lore, a bloody battle once took place between the Greek Sky God and the Cyclops. Afterward the triumphant Sky God sent his vanquished enemies to Hades, a place below the earth guarded by the Hound of Hell. When it came to hell and its denizens, the Gentiles displayed more passion and imagination than did the ancient Hebrews.

[83]

Alice K. Turner, author of "The History of Hell," points out that the ancient Jews had no expectation of seeing Yahweh after they died. Unlike neighboring cultures, they did not anticipate any sort of afterlife. This was certainly true through the days of Abraham and Moses, and even during the golden era of King David. A reading of Psalm 88:5 bears this out:

"Adrift among the dead, Like the slain who lie in the grave, Whom You remember no more, And who are cut off from your hand."

After exposure to outside influences, a Jewish afterlife concept gradually evolved. Isaiah 26:14,19 hints that Gentiles would have no afterlife but Yahweh's "dead shall live." By the time Daniel was written, circa 200 BCE, a Jewish belief in both eternal punishment and eternal reward is evident (Daniel 12:2-3). In the Jewish Apocrypha, dating from roughly the time of Daniel, there are images of a place of eternal torment and a furnace of hell.

Hell's most prominent citizen also changed over time. Seen by fundamentalists as the snake in the Garden of Eden, Satan (known as Lucifer before his fall from grace) helped lead humanity to estrangement from God. But a Satan who works consistently against God is not to be found in the Old Testament. Rather, we find a somewhat shady servant of Yahweh who is willing to get his hands dirty for the cause. Among other things, we find Satan acting on Yahweh's behalf as the destroyer of Egyptian children (Exodus 12:23), and as a spirit of ill will between Prince Abimelech and the men of Shechem (Judges 9:23). Perhaps most famously, God and Satan agree at the beginning of the Book of Job to test and torment a man Yahweh himself calls "a blameless and upright man (Job 1:8)."

By the time of Jesus, Satan had become his own boss, and God's clear adversary. In the gospels, Jesus is both tempted by Satan and confronted by him and his demons. By that time Satan was generally viewed by Jews as the head of a force of evil spirits. Some Jewish groups of the first century, such as the Pharisees, believed in a literal hell. Others, like the Sadducees, did not.

Hell, Satan and Christianity

The New Testament gospels provide a very imbalanced outlook on the threat of a literal hell. Mark, the first one written, is full of confrontation between Jesus and demonic spirits. At the same time he makes only one reference to hell (Mark 9:42-48). The last of the four to be written, the Gospel of John, does not specifically mention it at all. Luke does- but still only three times. This leaves us with a total of four references to hell in three complete gospels.

Matthew, on the other hand, repeatedly emphasizes hell in his Jewish-oriented gospel. Since the cursed Pharisees believed in literal fire and brimstone, Matthew's Jesus condemns them in terms they could relate to. Even so, this gospel describes the damned being punished in two completely different and inconsistent places. Matthew 13:42 and 13:50 show eternal misery in a furnace of fire, while Matthew 8:12, 22:13 and 25:30 place punishment for sinners in a place of outer darkness.

For the first few centuries after the time of Jesus, church leaders could not agree on the fate of unrepentant sinners. While Origen (185-254 CE) was teaching in Caesarea that all souls would eventually experience salvation, Tertullian (160-225 CE) promised eternal suffering for the damned. Tertullian's view prevailed after Christianity became Rome's imperial religion in 380 CE. This was due in no small part to help the state control the masses of a declining empire.

The venerable Augustine (354-430) created the Catholic view of hell, which was embraced by the Protestant fathers over a thousand years later. Augustine decided that hell is a material fire which torments the bodies of the damned for eternity. This place of permanent torture was a favorite object of literature, art and drama from the Dark and Middle Ages. The best known of such works is Dante's Inferno, an explicit description of hell produced around 1315. Dante's imagery found its way into both art and theology and gained wide acceptance as truth among the frightened masses of Europe.

The Protestant Reformation in no way dampened Christianity's zest for damming sinners to an eternity of punishing fire. Martin Luther, while rejecting the Catholic teaching of purgatory, spoke of a terrible and eternal hell. The Catholic Church itself issued a statement in 1870 affirming the permanent punishment of the damned in hell. While enlightened Christians abandoned such notions long ago, fundamentalists continue promoting fire and brimstone as enthusiastically as the Catholic Church of the Dark Ages.

Like godmen rising from the dead and hell itself , the concept of heaven has a pagan pedigree. An ancient Jewish belief in eternity with God in the sky did not exist, but by the time of Jesus the Jewish Pharisees did embrace the notion (the Sadducees did not). Among Gentiles exposed to Greek philosophy, belief in heaven enjoyed wide popularity.

The references to heaven in the New Testament paint a wide variety of images. Among them: it is like a mustard seed (Matthew 13:31); a treasure hidden in a field (Matthew 13: 44) and the Kingdom of the Father (Matthew 13:43). As one would expect from the strange Book of Revelation, a variety of odd images of heaven are offered- included among them: a throne with a God sitting on it who looks like "a jasper and a sardius stone (Revelation 4:2-3)." Heaven is also said to be home to "ten thousand times ten thousand (of) every creature which is in heaven and on the earth and under the earth (Revelation 5:12-13)." These are not the popular images of heaven which have been summarized as "people standing around in the clouds with wings on their back." As with hell, this impression comes mostly from European art of the Middle Ages and Renaissance.

The devil, so the story goes, has lived at both ends of the mythological spectrum. With scattered fragments from the Old and New

Testaments Satan's story has been patched together. Ezekiel 28:14-16 talks about a being who began as an "anointed Cherub." Despite the chapter being addressed to the King of Tyre, those finding the devil described in Ezekiel find that Satan was once perfect in his ways, sinned and was cast out of heaven.

The Overstory tells us that Lucifer and Satan are one and the same, and Isaiah 14:12 says "how far you have fallen from heaven, O Lucifer...You who weakened the nations." Moving to the New Testament, Jesus mentions Satan falling "like lightning from heaven (Luke 10:18)." This fall is described in Revelation 12:7-9 as a battle in heaven between Satan's angels and those of Michael. Satan's group lost and he and his fallen angels were cast to the earth.

The Overstory tells us that Satan's future can be seen in the twentieth chapter of Revelation. He will spend 1000 years in a bottomless pit, then be released for a little while (Revelation 20:3). After leading a final unsuccessful battle against God the evil one will be cast into a lake of fire and tormented forever (Revelation 20:10). And, so the story goes, that is the last time God will be dealing with the devil.

Every little ego-me in an Overstory-promoting church finds protection from the fear of an eternity in hell. Fundamentalist leaders dictate such a sentence for all who dare think differently than they do. The frightening irony is this: In the nuclear age myth, superstition and fear combined with humanity's modern ability to destroy itself could create something very hellish indeed.

CHAPTER 6
BRAINS LEFT BEHIND

Beyond The Armageddon Agenda

Before we get to the end, let's go back to the beginning. The creation of the entire universe is completely explained in just over one page of the Book of Genesis. While it is ridiculous to insist upon a "God said it, I believe it, and that settles it" outlook on the matter in the face of modern science, at least what fundamentalists claim as fact is clear and straightforward.

Understanding God's supposed plan to bring an end to history is a different matter altogether. After insisting on blind acceptance of ancient folklore concerning the earth's creation, the fundamentalists switch gears and tell us that future events are described in the Bible with hazy symbolic language. And this is from the same people who tell us that a literal interpretation of the entire Bible is the only way to avoid spending eternity in hell!

What a person believes is his or her personal business as long as those beliefs don't harm or threaten others. Unfortunately for those of us not accepting the Overstory, the end of the world scenario promoted by some of our neighbors crosses a line which makes their teachings everyone's concern. The supposed order of events is not clear and there are broad differences within the Armageddonist community about the specific details of what they expect to happen. Nevertheless, Christian fundamentalists almost universally believe that a final battle between the forces of good (people who think like they do) and evil (those who think differently) is imminent. Sharing the earth's resources with countless millions of people convinced that these are our final days is a serious problem. The situation is aggravated by their belief that the onset of World War III will usher Jesus down from the sky.

I read the entire Bible twice during my three years as a fundamentalist, but the Book of Revelation and it's so-called related prophecy was never an area of special interest to me. In fact, Revelation's dark tone and Alice-in-Wonderland style jabberwocky made me leave the matter in the hands of Christians of "greater discernment." More recent study has convinced me that the Armageddonists who claim to know what they are talking about have already had their brains raptured to a place far away from their mouths. Nevertheless, I have answered the questions which follow as objectively as possible:

1. How does the Overstory end?

2. Where did these notions come from?

3. Haven't Christians always expected the end of the world?

4. Is there a reasonable interpretation of the Book of Revelation?

5. What should a sane person do about the Armageddon agenda?

THE CONCLUSION OF THE OVERSTORY

In 1995 ultra-right wing Pastor Tim LaHaye and sportswriter Jerry Jenkins began producing their immensely popular "Left Behind" series. Sixteen adult titles (not counting related novels for young readers) and over 65 million total sales later, anticipation of the so-called rapture is even more popular among fundamentalists than before this fiction series was written. LaHaye's story line centers on people who remain earthbound during the rapture's aftermath. While promoted as fiction, Left Behind highlights an overstory within the Overstory.

The so-called art of interpreting Bible prophecy is really nothing more than forcing human imagination upon random bits of writing which were included in various parts of the Bible. The following seven entries provide an overview of near future events anticipated by our fundamentalist friends and neighbors:

One: Some Unmistakable Signs

Jesus told his disciples that the following signals would tell the world that the end is about to come: wars and rumors of wars, nations in distress, famines, epidemics and earthquakes in various places (Matthew 24:1-22; Mark 13:3-23; Luke 21:5-28). But when in the past two thousand years haven't these signs been present? This is one reason that Christians have been in the end times every day since Jesus was crucified.

Jesus specifically predicted to the disciples that his generation "will by no means pass away" before his second coming (Mark 13:30). He admitted that "of that day and hour no one knows, not even the angels in heaven, nor the Son, but only the Father (Mark 13:32)." The presence of these passages in the gospels reveals two things: first, that by the time the Gospel of Mark was written (circa 75 CE) the delay in Jesus' return was already a source of restlessness. Second, Jesus had not yet been promoted to full God status among Christians when this was written- how could you be God and not know what God knows?

Two: In Case of Rapture

We now jump to the letters of Paul for the next piece of the puzzle. Over 20 years after Jesus was crucified the apostle addressed worry over the fate of Christians who had died during the surprisingly long time that Jesus had been away. In I Thessalonians 4:16-17 Paul creatively shared "the dead in Christ will rise first. Then we who are alive and remain shall be caught up together with them in the clouds to meet the Lord in the air." This is not the second coming of Christ. Jesus does not touch ground during this episode which has come to be called the rapture. Oddly, the term rapture does not appear in the Bible and did not exist until the nineteenth century. Of course Paul anticipated that his own generation would witness the end of time as Jesus had promised.

Three: A Seven Year Tribulation

Before moving on, let's review some fundamentalist basics: When Genesis tells us that God created the universe in six days, those are literal days. But when Jesus told his disciples that he would return to earth within a generation, that did not mean a biblical generation of 40 years. Nearly 2000 years have since passed, so he obviously used the word "generation" in a symbolic way. Welcome to the end of Overstory. It gets a lot wilder, so strap yourself in.

As colorful as they are, fundamentalist "experts in prophecy" outdo even themselves in their use of the Old Testament's Book of Daniel. The 70 weeks mentioned in Daniel 9:24 have been changed in some recently-produced Bibles to "seventy sets of seven years." The first 69 of them supposedly ran between the time of Daniel and the crucifixion of Jesus. The counting stopped after that (say the Overstory experts) and the last seven years will start as soon as Israel signs a peace treaty with the Antichrist. This is said to be predicted in Daniel 9:26-27 and has not happened yet.

Daniel's soon to come final seven period has been named the tribulation, a term not from Daniel but pulled out of the Gospel of Matthew. It's details are not found in Daniel either- they are from the Book of Revelation. Spread out in Revelation chapters 4 through 19 in confusing and obscure language, readers are supposedly told what this tribulation has in store. Using hazy references to seven seals, seven trumpets and seven bowls the imaginative author of this book (said to be the Apostle John but more likely a Christian from Ephesus known as John the Elder) describes a supposedly loving God's horrific and spiteful revenge. It includes fiery red horses (Revelation 6:4), aggressive poisonous locusts with faces like men (Revelation 9:7) and oceans turning to blood (Revelation 16:3).

Four: All-Powerful God's Powerful Foe

John the Elder (or whoever wrote Revelation) weaved a frightening tale. For good measure he added a villain but didn't provide us the name he is known by. For that, one must jump to the First and Second Epistles of John. There the word "antichrist" is used four times- and it is found nowhere else in the Bible.

According to the Overstory the Antichrist will appear to be a hero for the first half of the tribulation. Halfway through the seven years he will show his true colors, be killed but then resurrected by Satan. This is supposedly revealed through a sea monster story in Revelation, Chapter 13. The Antichrist is also expected to take on a false prophet as his personal assistant. This evil sidekick will administer the infamous "666" mark which will be necessary for all commerce.

Five: Welcome to Armageddon

According to our fundamentalist friends, the Antichrist will lead a military force against an army from the east in the Battle of Armageddon. The battle's name comes from Revelation 16:16, its details from a patchwork of passages from both testaments. They include Zechariah, Jeremiah, Jude and (of course) Revelation. Read literally, the relevant passages amount to an incoherent ramble. There are frogs emerging from the mouth of a dragon (Revelation 16:13), jackals and wild desert beasts (Jeremiah 50:39) and confused horses with mad riders (Zechariah 12:4). While these clues might not mean a lot to reasonable minds, to the discerning eye of the Overstory zealot they reveal God's unbending truth.

Roughly speaking, what they expect is like this: A ten nation alliance led by the Antichrist will assemble at Armageddon with the idea of destroying Israel. After opposing forces from the east destroy Babylon the Antichrist will conquer Jerusalem, kill a great number of Jews, and head south to annihilate those who escape. These Jews, however, will pray to Jesus before the Antichrist can kill them. Jesus will then return from heaven with an army of angels and Christian saints. This scenario has been crudely patched together by the so-called experts with passages from Daniel, Zechariah, Jude and, again, Revelation.

Six: It's About Time He Got Here

Jesus' long-anticipated second coming (supposedly described in Revelation 19:11-16) is different from the rapture. The second coming will happen later, and this time Jesus will make it all the back to earth. He will bind Satan for 1000 years (Revelation 20:1-3) and then rule our planet personally. Things will then go smoothly until Satan's final comeback attempt at end of the ten centuries.

Seven: Lest Ye Be Judged

After Satan has served his thousand year prison term he will gather an army and attempt to fight for Jerusalem. The devil will fail and then face judgment with his demons. God will cast them into hell for eternity (Revelation 20:7-10), the same fate which awaits non-believers after they have been convicted by Jesus in front of his great white throne (Revelation 20:11-15). Most of our fundamentalist friends will already be in heaven by this time, having passed through the pearly gates after the rapture.

Following the above seven episodes, eternity will be underway. Hallelujah!

THE ORIGIN OF ARMAGEDDON MYTHOLOGY

As we have seen, much of the Overstory comes from mythology which is older than Christianity and sometimes older than Judaism. Not surprisingly, the end-of-the-world "Left Behind" mentality of the religious right came from outside as well. It's roots are found in Zoroastrianism, a religion which was dominant in Persia and the greater Middle East from about 550 BCE until the arrival of Islam during the seventh century CE. This faith still has an estimated 250,000 followers today. One of its core teachings is that good will ultimately destroy evil at the end of time. A final judgment of all souls will then take place with Saoshyant, the Zoroastrian Savior, resurrecting the bodies of all good people. If all of this sounds familiar, it should.

The Zoroastrians introduced eschatology, the supposed ability to predict events leading to the end of history, into Western religion. By 200 BCE, a Zoroastrian influence on Judaism was well established. A universe of light versus darkness, angels versus demons, and God versus a powerful enemy can be traced directly to these ancient Persians. This concept was accepted by a significant number of Jews during the last few centuries before the birth of Jesus.

Christianity reflects a great deal of Zoroastrian influence. Jesus, rather than Saoshyant, is the figure who will usher in the end of time. The second chapter of Matthew has three Magi (or "wise men") in its Christmas narrative. Scholars recognize them as Zoroastrian astrologers following the signs of their own faith as they seek out the baby Jesus. At the other end of the New Testament, the Book of Revelation provides a distorted rehash of the Zoroastrian showdown between good and evil. Zoroastrianism is the very obvious source of Christian Armageddon mythology.

IS IT OVER YET?

Christianity has creatively updated it's never-ending end times scenario as necessary over the past 2000 years. In fact, the end of history now has a very long and colorful history of its own. During the first century such expectations were brought about by the very words of Jesus. When he failed to come back within a generation as he had promised, the end times speculation we still experience was underway. Since the end of the first century, hundreds of dates have been set and then abandoned by Christians supposedly in the know.

Around the year 200 Hippolytus, one of the most respected writers in the early Church, became convinced that those present in the year 500 would witness the return of Jesus. Some 300 years later those buying into his formula were, of course, disappointed. For all of the final days fever Hippolytus whipped up around the year 500 it paled compared to the apocalyptic obsession later attached to the year 1000. European Christians became widely convinced that January 1, 1000 would be the day that Jesus returned. Many gave their worldly goods to the Church in anticipation of the end of the world. Apparently their donations were generally not returned when their expectations failed to materialize.

The period from 1001 to 1500 saw it's share of Armageddon speculation as well. As soon as Christendom shook off the disappointment of Jesus' failure to return in 1000, many became convinced that 1033, a date seen as 1000 years after Jesus' death and resurrection, would provide the second coming. Pope Innocent III, who led the Church from 1198 until 1216, predicted that the end would come in 1284 (he added 666 to the year that Islam was founded).

The Black Plague ravaged Europe from 1346 to 1400, killing roughly one-third of its population. Christians became convinced that they were witnessing the epidemic and famine Jesus mentions in Matthew, Mark and Luke. After they were disappointed the year 1500 became the focus of speculation, just as had been the case with 500 and 1000. Another date certain, another certain disappointment.

The past 500 years have seen the tradition continue. Melchior Hoffman (1495-1543), an early Protestant leader and visionary, convinced a significant number of people in Holland and Germany that Jesus would return in 1533. Hoffman was arrested after this failed to happen and jailed in Strasbourg, Germany- the very place he had told his followers that the New Jerusalem would be established. 1689 was held up as doomsday by English Baptist minister and author Benjamin Keach, as was 1794 by Charles Wesley who co-founded England's Methodist movement.

The past two hundred years have been ripe with apocalyptic expectation. Some predictions, such as those offered by Mormon founder Joseph Smith and successive generations of Jehovah's Witnesses, are labeled as cult-oriented guesswork by fundamentalists. But those embracing the Overstory have had plenty of specific predictions come from within the fold. Perhaps the best known and most successful was in Hal Lindsey's 1970 bestseller "The Late Great Planet Earth" which has sold over 35 million copies. It predicted that the rapture would happen in 1988. Over two decades later, those who missed out on that faux-rapture bide their time and thrill to the "Left Behind" series.

I have some bad news and some good news. The bad news is that, according to the fundamentalist community, the end times are upon us. The good news is that, based upon 2000 years of consistently false expectations, the end can almost certainly be forestalled if humanity chooses to act in a reasonable manner.

REVELATION READ REASONABLY

It barely made the cut when the contents of the Bible were finally settled upon in 367 CE. Martin Luther, the founder of Protestantism, once said that "Christ is neither taught nor known in it." But combine the Book of Revelation with an Overstory zealot and you have a frightening combination of two things, both of which lack logical clarity.

Whoever wrote Revelation, for whatever reason, must have meant something by it. While some critics suspect that the book's author may have suffered from psychosis, that explanation doesn't stand up when this work is viewed beside similar Jewish and Christian writings from the period between 200 BCE and 200 CE. Revelation takes its place beside such lesser-known classics as the Apocalypse of Ezra, the Apocalypse of Paul, the Apocalypse of Peter and the Ascension of Isaiah. All owe much to their common ancestor, Zoroastrian mythology, for their colorful and frightening images.

Examining the Apocalypse of John (now better known as the Book of Revelation) as it appears in the Bible, the following conclusions are reasonable: It was written about 95 CE and promoted as the work of the Apostle John to enhance its credibility. Revelation was more likely composed by an Ephesian known as John the Elder. The book is anti-Roman in tone and refers to Rome, which destroyed Jerusalem in 70 CE, as "Babylon." This is a symbolic reference to the earlier conquering power which razed the Jewish temple in 587 BCE. Revelation also mimics the tone of Old Testament prophecy by appearing to predict events which had actually occurred some 25 years before it was written.

The period of tribulation described in chapters 4 through 19 of Revelation is a veiled reference to the Roman siege of Jerusalem between 68 and 70 CE. The city's walls were barricaded by the Jews inside creating the fear, desperation and famine described. When Roman soldiers finally breached Jerusalem's walls they ransacked the city and destroyed the temple. Vespasian was the Roman emperor in power at the time of the fall of the holy city in the year 70, but the period from 54-68 CE saw the reign of the dreaded Nero. Not surprisingly, the Greek form of his name (Neron Caesar) carries the numerical equivalent of "666" when written in Hebrew characters.

I have offered as reasonable an explanation of the Book of Revelation as can be given. It is odd, but not unique among the writings of its time. It is one of many apocalyptic works written after the Roman destruction of Jerusalem in 70 CE. Masquerading as already-fulfilled prophecy, Revelation was meant to inspire an early Christian community which obsessed about Jesus' failure to come back to earth by 95 CE.

SANTITY AND THE ARMAGEDDON AGENDA

Not long ago an acquaintance asked me "do you think these are the end times?" I responded that they could be, depending on the choices humanity makes. Just as Overstory zealots require a literal reading of Genesis while at the same time insisting upon a symbolic interpretation of Revelation, a similar contradiction presents itself with the issue of free will. Humanity is said to be estranged from God because Adam and Eve exercised this freedom against the advice of their creator. On the other hand, terrible things are supposedly about to happen to all of us, and the Overstory tells us there isn't a thing we can do about it. But we can! In the face of those promoting the Armageddon agenda, you have the right (I view it as a duty) to reject this disturbed fundamentalist doomsday outlook. Here are some suggestions:

Just Say No to the Armageddon Agenda

Again, the Overstory tells us that the mess we are in is strictly due to humanity's abuse of God's gift of free will. Tell your fundamentalist friends that God is seeing if we are now smart enough to use our freedom to avert disaster. If everyone just says no to participating in any sort of religious violence, Armageddon can never happen! Otherwise we have no choice, no free will and we are nothing but pawns in an angry creator's perverse form of amusement.

Discuss "God's Enemies"

First, have the Overstory zealot take a reasonable look at the Satan character he or she believes in. On one hand, the devil is cagy enough to tempt people away from God in subtly deceptive ways. On the other hand, he is too stupid to read Bible prophecy and change his future plans accordingly. It can't be too tough to make adjustments on game day when the other team's play book is wide open. Or is Satan just another pawn without free will in the Overstory God's pre-programmed drama?

Patiently point out that a combination of holy writings, inspiring leadership and regular fellowship does not make the Overstory true. The same exact components are in place among Muslim fundamentalists who themselves insist that Christians are in the grip of Satan!

Recommend This Book

While it may be a long shot, pass an Overstory fundamentalist your copy of this book. I once thought just like they do- and this book patiently explains why I no longer do. Remember that the Manson family acted upon their leader's interpretation of the Book of Revelation armed only with rope, knives and a pistol. While a terrible tragedy, their actions will pale compared to what the leader of a nuclear power could do armed the Overstory. In all honesty such a thought occurred to me more than once during the years of Dick Cheney and George W. Bush. Still, thankfully, it's not the end of the world unless humanity decides that it is.

CHAPTER 7
IT QUACKS LIKE A CULT

Beyond Fire, Brimstone and Right-Wing Propaganda

Up to this point I have tried to shine a light on the frequently false and threatening components of the fundamentalist Overstory. In chapter one I used the Hundred Mile Walk as a metaphor to illustrate Christianity's net negative influence on Western history. At this time I would like to introduce another metaphor, Overstory pizza. I will then review what was served up on Sunday morning at several fundamentalist churches in my area.

The one item not available at Overstory outlets is plain cheese pizza. For our purposes, plain cheese pizza is pure enlightened spirituality, the kind Jesus shared when he told us to love our neighbors as ourselves. At the outlets I visited, various combinations of the toppings listed below were generally heaped upon whatever cheese might have been hidden underneath:

OVERSTORY PIZZA TOPPINGS

1. False History

2. Book Idolatry

3. Mythology

4. Superstition

5. Fear

6. Right-Wing Politics

7. Spiritual Bigotry

8. Armageddon Insanity

During the spring and summer of 2008 I sampled six different Overstory Pizza outlets in the San Diego area. Some outlets were spicier and more generous with their toppings than others. I created a rating system reflecting this fact: A rating of "10" would indicate generous portions of deep-dish Overstory insanity. A "1" would be your basic enlightened cheese pizza. On that basis the lowest (closest to enlightened) rating at any of the churches I visited was a delightfully surprising "3" but it got frightfully spicier from there. In order of the dates I visited, the fare served up was as follows:

Mission Valley Christian Fellowship
San Diego, CA

I returned to my former church on Sunday March 3, 2008 in order to take in the 9:30am service. The program started off with a short set of feel-good Jesus songs played by a combo calling itself the Sunday Drivers. Leo Giovinetti, my former pastor, then took the stage. He plugged his church's family ministry, bragging that "our kids are on-fire little evangelists" before adding that "the devil is after each successive generation." On a roll with the topic of family, Pastor Leo plugged his upcoming appearance on former San Diego mayor Roger Hedgecock's right-wing radio talk show. Giovenetti promised to use the opportunity to call attention to "the homosexual agenda."

After a quick sales pitch for Pastor Leo's Holy Roast Coffee, an apparently popular fundraiser introduced since I left his church, the morning's scripture-laced sermon was underway. It was certainly not in harmony with the good news hymns I had heard just a few minutes before. The pastor drew our attention to Isaiah 13:6 which reads "the day of the Lord...will come as destruction from the Almighty." He reinforced his angry theme with passages such as

Revelation 12:7, which begins "and war broke out in heaven." Pastor Leo was quick to remind the crowd that "if there is war in heaven there will be war on earth despite the misguided efforts of the peaceniks."

We were told in closing to "serve the Lord because the alternative is horrible." As the service ended all in attendance were encouraged to "register to vote in the back (and) hold the City Council's feet to the fire."

House Specialty: Holy War Combo (Toppings 2, 4, 5, 6, 8)
Overall Rating: 9 (generous, spicy portions heaped on)

Foothills Christian Church
El Cajon, CA

When I arrived for the 8:30am service on Sunday March 16, 2008 I was immediately struck with the appearance of the sanctuary. It looked like a television sound stage, providing the house band with a great venue to play its string of praise songs. When the music ended and Pastor David Hoffman arrived at his podium a right-wing tirade was underway as soon as he had opened his mouth. The first order of business was a prayer for "our troops serving Jesus in 30 countries" and a reminder that "Christians have a duty to vote- especially against the gay agenda." Hoffman bemoaned the fact that his opposition to homosexuality could be labeled hate speech by a sinful world.

The topic of the morning's main sermon was "Do You Want to Know God?" I could not help but answer in my mind "not if he is as bigoted as you are." In fairness to my hosts, the sermon was easier to listen to than the introductory messages had been. In fact, the irony of some of the pastor's points did not go unnoticed. One of them was that God is actually inside of us. That valid, if misunderstood, assertion was the best of a lot which went quickly downhill from there. Some of the other power points included the opinion that the Bible is God's opinion and an intolerant slam against all who dare embrace a truth other than Hoffman's: "when other religions ask God to speak to them someone does- and its sure not God."

The service ended with a loud rebuke to closet internet pornography surfers and a reminder to sign right-wing political petitions on the way out of church. I declined.

House Specialty: Right-Wing Propaganda Lover's Pizza
(Toppings 2, 4, 6 and 7)
Overall Rating: 9 (deep-dish, hearty and spicy)

Pathways Community Church
Santee, CA

After the fare served at the previous two churches I had visited the 9:00am service on March 30, 2008 at Pathways was a comparatively enlightened oasis. The sanctuary is a converted supermarket now set up like a TV sound stage, only on a tighter budget than the one I had seen at Foothills Christian Church. A younger and somewhat edgier-sounding worship band played the perfunctory half-dozen or so offerings, after which Pastor Phil Herrington began his sermon which was entitled "Detours on the Highway of Life."

After reminding all in attendance to love our neighbors as ourselves Pastor Herrington talked about a recent church mission to Mexico. His church had built houses for people living in grinding poverty. Explaining that God wanted these poor people to have more than what very little they do, the pastor asked us to seriously consider that these people are our neighbors in exactly the way that Jesus had intended in his famous statement about love. He then reminded all in attendance that when God puts detours in our lives, they are frequently opportunities to serve others. Other than the superstitious premise that a separate God is interacting individually with well over six billion human egos, the service was delightful.

House Specialty: Sweet but Superstitious Pizza
(laced with Topping 4)
Overall Rating: 3 (I could actually taste the cheese!)

Sonrise Community Church
Santee, CA

Following my pleasant experience at Pathways just three weeks earlier, I entered Sonrise Community Church at 9:00am on Sunday April 20, 2008 with guarded optimism. It was set up in the cookie-cutter sound stage style, but on a grander scale. Sporting an orchestra of about 30 souls to compliment a choir of some 50 more, the 500 or so in attendance had every right to expect some prime-time spiritual entertainment. In a highly perverse sense it was delivered, but even my worst suspicions about Overstory Christianity could not have prepared me for what I was about to hear.

After the singing had ended, a guest speaker was introduced. His name was Lou Engle and he was more than up to his task. A smoky-voiced man of about 55 years, Engle rocked back and forth as he shared his message. The founder of a hyper-right wing ministry known as The Call, he was nothing if not disturbing. Pastor Engle's observations included:

"There is a generation born for extremism and we must let them burn for God."

"God took 625,000 lives in the Civil War to end slavery. Imagine how many lives he is going to have to take to end abortion."

"Pray to end the abortion movement and the prophet Elijah will bring us something radical."

"Prayer and fasting can end sexual addiction and homosexuality."

"God blessed us with George W. Bush and two judges to end partial birth abortion."

"God's actual voice awoke me at 4:00 am to tell me that he is ready to turn America around."

What was perhaps most frightening were hundreds of my neighbors apparently in agreement with Engle's views. At the end of the sermon their regular pastor, Tony Foglio, endorsed his guest speaker as "a man for times like these."

[105]

House Specialty: Nut House Delight
(smothered in Toppings 1, 3, 4, 5, 6 and 7)
Overall Rating: 10 (but only because that
is the highest number allowed)

Journey Community Church
La Mesa, CA

Nearly three months after my disturbing experience at Sonrise I finally ventured forth to sample more local Overstory fare. Visiting Journey Community Church's 9:00am service on Sunday July 13, 2008 I had no idea what to expect based on the broad differences in the churches I had visited in March and April. Would I be treated to the golden rule approach of Pathways, the frightening lunacy of Sonrise or something in-between? Journey turned out to be a big improvement over Sonrise (anything short of human sacrifice would have been) but it was not quite the best of the lot I sampled.

As always, a praise band set the service in motion. They were followed by the sermon of a guest speaker, Christian author Don Everts. His message concerned what he called growth in the Kingdom of God. Personable and youthful (apparently in his late thirties) Everts told the crowd that conversion to Christianity is the first step in an essential growth, and shared stories about his patient and kind efforts to lead a neighbor to Christ. The author also shared a strong conviction that God speaks to us in our dreams. While the presentation was civil and non-threatening it still underscored the softer side of spiritual bigotry. That, paraphrased, is "if you don't share my ideas about God, it is my duty to change your thinking."

House Specialty: Polite Proselytizer's Pizza (Toppings 4 and 7)
Overall Rating: 5

Horizon Christian Fellowship
San Diego, CA

The 11:00am service at Horizon Christian Fellowship on Sunday

July 20, 2008 was my final church service. Christian recording artist Jimmy Robeson opened the now very familiar pop culture worship format served up at all of the churches I visited. Much like the Sonrise experience in April, the general "Jesus is wonderful" tone of the music was followed by some fanatic fire and brimstone preaching.

Pastor Mike McIntosh, a man frequently credited with bringing the Jesus Movement to San Diego in the 1970s, delivered the sermon. His theme for the morning was biblical proof of a literal hell and some specifics about what it is like. McIntosh began with what he called proof of hell's existence by reading Proverbs 15:24: "The way of life winds upward for the wise, that he may turn away from hell below."

The next order of business was letting the gathering know what this hell is like. "People in hell this morning are remembering the sinful things they did with you, or to you," the pastor intoned. He added that people in hell can hear, think, reason and feel despite the fact that these damned souls don't have a body. It is the price individuals and nations who reject Jesus must pay, McIntosh shared, adding that "the United States has turned away from God" and "we must get ready for the final judgment." As I left I felt relieved that I would not soon again be listening to Mike McIntosh or his ilk.

House Specialty: Demon's Delicacy
(The Works-all eight toppings piled on)
Overall Rating: 9

All in all, I heard an angrier message at these six churches than the one I recall from my days as a regular attendee. That being said, it is important to emphasize that many groups who also claim to teach the Bible are not in harmony with the core components of the fundamentalist Overstory. Those groups are frequently derided as cults.

It should go without saying that groups not practicing Bible book idolatry (Buddhists, Hindus, Muslims, Zen practitioners, etc) are considered unworthy of the mercy of the Overstory God. But also included on the fundamentalist blacklist are many groups also claiming biblical salvation. They include:

The Roman Catholic Church

Long villainized by Protestants, by the mid-twentieth century a thaw between the Roman Catholic Church and mainstream Protestantism was underway. But since that time the influence of the mainline sects (Episcopal, Lutheran, Presbyterian, etc.) has been seriously eroded by Overstory fundamentalism and the Catholic Church is again widely viewed as a cult. The reasons include Catholic allegiance to the Pope, prayers to Mary and confession of individual sins to priests. Fundamentalists don't advertise the fact that the early Roman Church selected the books of the New Testament and did not do so until nearly 400 CE.

Mormonism

This relatively recent group began in nineteenth century America and features several teachings and practices which are ridiculed by fundamentalists. Despite undeniable success in the area of "traditional family values," the Church of Jesus Christ of Latter-day Saints teaches that good Mormons can one day become gods themselves. They also sometimes baptize the dead and have a volume which is equal to the Bible, the Book of Mormon. A Jewish friend once remarked to me "the Book of Mormon is to Jesus freaks what the New Testament is to a Jew."

Christian Science

Also a product of the United States of the 1800s, Christian Science is another faith which has earned Overstory cult status. Like the Mormons, this group has a companion volume to the Bible, Mary Baker Eddy's "Science and Health." The fact that the group prays to a "Father-Mother God" and denies the existence of the devil is a threat to those needing a powerful foe to battle their supposedly all-powerful God.

Seventh-Day Adventists

At this point it may not surprise you that the Seventh-day Adventists also trace their roots to the America of the 1800s. This church with an estimated 8 million adherents worships on Saturdays, teaches that Jesus is Michael the Archangel and that human sin will ultimately be placed upon Satan. The Adventists have thereby earned the Overstory cult designation.

Jehovah's Witnesses

Jehovah's Witnesses are like the Mormons, Christian Scientists and Seventh-day Adventists in that they too emerged from (you probably guessed it) the nineteenth century United States. Unlike the Mormons and Scientists, however, Jehovah's Witnesses use only the Bible, study it judiciously and arrive at conclusions different to those taught by the Overstory fundamentalists.

The Witnesses are particularly loathed by the modern pop culture Jesus Movement for concluding that God is only one person, Jehovah (Yahweh), and not a Trinity. Jesus is viewed by the group as a perfect man who was not God in the flesh. The Holy Spirit is taught to be an impersonal active force. The fact that reading the Bible could lead to a different theology than the one promoted by the Overstory (I offered three of them in chapter four) is especially threatening to fundamentalists. They claim that Jehovah's Witnesses, like all "cults," are in the grip of Satan.

[109]

I recently went to the website of Foothills Christian Church for a clear statement of core Overstory teachings. I found out that the devil runs from true Christians (James 4:7). I was also informed that death is not to be feared and if it happens before Jesus returns the faithful will immediately be present with him (II Corinthians 5:6-8). Those alive when Jesus returns are promised a meeting with him in the clouds (I Thessalonians 4:16-17).

The Cult of the Month Club present in America did not end in 1900. My recent Sunday visits are a testimony to the fact that creative religious fanaticism is alive and well right here in my own backyard. My grandmother used to tell me "if it waddles like a duck and it quacks like a duck it is probably a duck." The same would hold true with cults.

CHAPTER 8
FOCUS ON THE BIGOTRY

Some Questions and Answers

During the course of the writing of this book, friends and some who were not so friendly posed a number of legitimate questions. Some of them are quoted verbatim below while others have been paraphrased to represent certain types of inquiries I heard more than once.

What is the point of "Beyond Spiritual Bigotry?"

To encourage people to slow down, take a deep breath and think things over before diving over the cliff of Armageddon insanity. And, of course, to get people to focus on the bigoted and dangerous aspects of some supposedly positive teachings.

Aren't you bigoted against fundamentalism yourself?

I am only intolerant of intolerance. I don't oppose the Ku Klux Klan because I'm against white people but because of the bigotry the Klan promotes. The same applies to Overstory fundamentalists. I don't oppose their spirituality. I oppose the fact that they sneer at the spirituality of everyone who thinks differently than they do. All spiritual outlooks are entitled to equal respect- provided they extend the same respect to others.

Don't fundamentalists have the right to free speech?

Certainly, as do all bigoted individuals and groups. It is the duty of others to point out that bigotry is not to be endorsed, and should be opposed by enlightened people.

Are you against Jesus?

Not at all. I embrace the teachings of the legitimate Jesus of history. At the same time I reject the fictitious Overstory spun by misguided individuals who have twisted the teachings of Jesus out of all reasonable context. The historical Jesus was enlightened, brilliant, pacifistic, non-materialistic and politically alienated. In other words, he had nothing in common with the modern so-called Christian fundamentalists who praise his name while running roughshod over his teachings.

Don't fundamentalist churches
help people to solve their problems?

To be sure, the counseling offered to people with regard to their life situations can be beneficial. But whatever benefit is gained does not validate the Overstory, and especially the bigotry which comes with it.

Don't fundamentalist churches help
people break addictions?

Freedom from drugs, alcohol and other unhealthy activities and substances are a very important focus. Bigotry and Armageddon insanity, however, are problems just like substance abuse and are not attached to the recovery process in a truly spiritual environment. The most successful methods of recovery insist upon universal tolerance.

My pastor teaches what you call the Overstory,
but isn't he an expert on God?

Quite the contrary, he is an expert on the Overstory.

Why is what other people believe any of your business?

It isn't- unless it threatens me and the planet I live on and/or disrespects the legitimate spirituality of everyone else.

Shouldn't I take my children to church to learn family values?

If you like, provided the church you take them to is made up of families who respect others. Frightening children by telling them that peaceful neighbors will be tortured in hell for living or thinking differently than they do is an insidious bigotry. It has no place in an enlightened family.

Isn't it because of Christianity that we
have more freedom than Islamic countries do?

That is a testimony to the strength of our secular society and the foresight of the founders of this country. They made sure that religious nuts could not have the run of our government through the First Amendment to the United States Constitution. If our religious kooks had the same level of influence as the Islamic lunatic fringe does in many places America would have a one-way ticket back to the Dark Ages.

Why don't you write a book criticizing radical Islam?

While that is certainly a worthwhile pursuit, I do not have the background to write such a book. I have not read much of the Koran, I have read the Bible from cover to cover twice. I have never had with any association with any form of Islam while for three years I was an active member of an Overstory-promoting fundamentalist Christian sect.

Just what do you mean by "the Overstory?"

The Overstory is a term I coined to describe the web of interdependent falsehoods, half truths, meaningless truths and superstitions used to prop up the fundamentalist faux reality. The first six chapters of this book discussed each of them separately.

Don't fundamentalist churches do a lot of valuable charity work?

However much legitimate, no strings attached charity work they are doing I urge them to continue. I also implore them with equal urgency to stop promoting spiritual bigotry.

Aren't you promoting a radical philosophy?

All I am asking is for people to stop being bigots and to stop threatening the planet that we all share. Is that really so radical?

Why don't you start an organization to
promote world peace and universal tolerance?

It is done. If you would like to help, look us up at
"http://www.focusonthebigotry.com/". Best wishes to you and yours.

SELECTED BIBLIOGRAPHY

Armstrong, Karen. A History of God. New York: Random House, 1993.

Armstrong, Karen. A Short History of Myth. Edinburgh, Scotland: Cannongate Books, 2005.

Bawer, Bruce. Stealing Jesus. New York: Three Rivers Press, 1997.

Bickel, Bruce and Jantz, Stan. Bible Prophecy 101. Eugene, OR: Harvest House Publishers, 1999.

Carmichael, Joel. The Birth of Christianity. New York: Dorset Press, 1989.

Chamberlain, Chuck. A New Pair of Glasses. Irvine, CA: New Look Publishing, 1984.

Ehrman, Bart. Misquoting Jesus. New York: HarperCollins Publishers, 2005.

Ellerbee, Linda. The Dark Side of Christian History. Orlando, FL: Morningstar & Lark, 1995.

Freke, Timothy and Gandy, Peter. The Jesus Mysteries. New York: Three Rivers Press, 1999.

The Holy Bible. New King James Version. Nashville: Thomas Nelson Publishers, 1982.

Klassen, Randy. What Does the Bible Really Say About Hell? Telford, PA: Pandora Press, 2001.

Leeming, David. Jealous Gods and Chosen People. New York: Oxford University Press, 2004.

Mc Dowell, Josh. The New Evidence That Demands a Verdict. Nashville: Thomas Nelson Publishers, 1999.

Mears, Henrietta C. What the Bible is All About. Minneapolis: World Wide Publications, 1966.

Nelson-Pallmeyer, Jack. Jesus Against Christianity. Harrisburg, PA: Trinity Press International, 2001.

The Other Bible. Edited by William Barnstone. New York: HarperCollins Publishers, 2005.

Spong, John Shelby: The Sins of Scripture. New York: HarperCollins Publishers, 2005.

Turner, Alice K. The History of Hell. Orlando, FL: Harcourt, Brace and Company, 1993.

Webb, Jeffrey B. The Complete Idiot's Guide to Exploring God. New York: Alpha Books, 2005.

White, L. Michael: From Jesus to Christianity. New York: HarperCollins Publishers, 2005.

Wharton, Gary C. Jesus The Authorized Biography. Green Forest, AR: New Leaf Press, 2005.

9 781432 722216